Oregon
BY THEME
DAY TRIPS

T0020881

Stacy McCullough

Adventure Publications
Cambridge, Minnesota

Safety Notice Oregon is home to a host of potentially dangerous animals including rattlesnakes, bears, and mountain lions, as well as natural hazards, such as extreme temperatures, avalanches, mudslides, bluffs, and drop-offs (not to mention the possibility of volcanic activity, earthquakes, and tsunamis). Always heed posted safety warnings, take commonsense safety precautions, and remain aware of your surroundings. *Remember:* You're responsible for your own safety.

For the latest information about destinations in this book that have been affected by the coronavirus, please check the phone numbers and websites in the trip profiles. For news and updates about the coronavirus in Oregon, see govstatus.egov.com/or-oha-covid-19.

Editors: Brett Ortler and Ritchey Halphen
Cover and book design by Jonathan Norberg

Front cover photo: Yaquina Head Lighthouse, Newport, OR: **Bob Pool/shutterstock.com;** map: **Globe Turner/shutterstock.com**
Back cover photo: **Alexander Oganezov/shutterstock.com**

Photos used under license from Shutterstock.com:
anthony kuempel: 126 (top); **Atlaspix:** 107 (flag front); **B Brown:** 31; **Bob Pool:** 6, 39, 117, 124 (bottom), 131; **Bonnie Fink:** 21; **Borka Kiss:** 107 (flag back); **Breck P. Kent:** 111 (top); **Christian Musat:** 110 (top); **CSNafzger:** 16, 98, 101, 109 (top); **Dancestrokes:** 124 (top); **davidrh:** 49; **Dee Browning:** 127 (top), 129; **Dené Miles:** 133; **dylan:** 104; **Edmund Lowe Photography:** 127 (bottom); **Eponaleah:** 70; **Eric Friedebach:** 78; **Eugene Kalenkovich:** 40; **f111photo:** 115; **Gabriela Dolezelova:** 122; **Gary Gilardi:** 118; **Hills Outdoors:** 121; **Hlewk:** 118; **Hugh K Telleria:** 108 (bottom); **Jack Bell Photography:** 109 (bottom); **Jeffrey T. Kreulen:** 130; **Jeremy Pawlowski:** 77; **Jon Bilous:** 10; **JPL Designs:** 84, 123 (bottom); **J.S. Brusatori:** 112 (top); **Kalona Photography:** 102; **Kateryna Kon:** 113 (bottom); **Leonid Andronov:** 62; **Marisa Estivill:** 15; **Michael 1123:** 125 (top); **Michael Schober:** 123 (top); **Michael Warwick:** 125 (bottom); **MISHELLA:** 89; **Nancy Bauer:** 112 (bottom); **Natalka De:** 108 (top); **Neil Lockhart:** 116; **Pung:** 114; **Ramblin Rod:** 126 (bottom); **Real Window Creative:** 32, 128; **Rigucci:** 132; **Robert Crow:** 50; **Robert Crum:** 106; **Robert Mutch:** 72; **Russ Heinl:** 69; **Ryan Kelehar:** 120 (bottom); **Sean Pavone:** 5; **Steve Byland:** 110 (bottom); **steve estvanik:** 53; **TFoxFoto:** 44, 83; **Thomas Barrat:** 54; **vectorissimo:** 107 (map); **Victoria Ditkovsky:** 120 (top)

These images are licensed under the Attribution 2.0 Generic (CC BY 2.0) license, which is available at https://creativecommons.org/licenses/by/2.0/: Cantharellus formosus by **Dick Culbert:** 111 (bottom), original image via: https://flickr.com/photos/92252798@N07/31054406704/; Baldwin Hotel by **Eric Friedebach:** 78, original image via https://flickr.com/photos/friedebach/51107107753/; Holiday Express by **Noël Zia Lee:** 90, original image via: https://flickr.com/photos/noelzialee/2111228215/

These images are licensed under the CC0 1.0 Universal (CC0 1.0) Public Domain Dedication license, which is available at https://creativecommons.org/publicdomain/zero/1.0/: B-25J at Evergreen Museum by **Karl Dickman:** 22; Oregon Hairy Triton by **NOAA:** 113 (top); Dug Bar by **Roger M. Peterson/USFWS:** 94

10 9 8 7 6 5 4 3 2 1

Oregon Day Trips by Theme
Copyright © 2021 by Stacy McCullough
Adventure Publications
An imprint of AdventureKEEN
310 Garfield Street South
Cambridge, Minnesota 55008
(800) 678-7006
www.adventurepublications.net
All rights reserved

ISBN 978-1-59193-928-3 (pbk.); ISBN 978-1-59193-929-0 (ebook)

Disclaimer Please note that travel information changes under the impact of many factors that influence the travel industry. We therefore suggest that you call ahead for confirmation when making your travel plans. Every effort has been made to ensure the accuracy of information throughout this book, and the contents of this publication are believed to be correct at the time of printing. Nevertheless, the publishers cannot accept responsibility for errors or omissions, for changes in details given in this guide, or for the consequences of any reliance on the information provided by the same. Assessments of attractions and so forth are based upon the author's own experiences; therefore, descriptions given in this guide necessarily contain an element of subjective opinion, which may not reflect the publisher's opinion or dictate a reader's own experience on another occasion.

Table of Contents

Dedication

To E, The gentlest soul I know and my lifelong hiking buddy.
All my love, sweet girl.

—Stacy McCullough

A Word About Admission

Some of the destinations and activities in this book cost nothing to experience, while others charge admission. Check the phone numbers and websites in the trip listings for the latest information.

For information about parking and day-use fees at **Oregon State Parks,** go to stateparks.oregon.gov; under "Visit," choose "Day-Use Parking Fees." The webpage also contains links to information about special passes that can be used at fee-charging national parks, forests, and recreation areas in Oregon.

Portland, Oregon, and Mt. Hood in the background

A barn owl at Sunriver Nature Center

FROM ITS FASCINATING and sometimes explosive geology to its often-pristine habitats and ecosystems, Oregon is a great place to explore the wonders of the natural world. There are hands-on opportunities for all ages to learn about geology, astronomy, and more throughout the state.

SCIENCE EXPLORATION

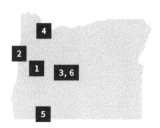

1 Eugene Science Center

2300 Leo Harris Parkway, Eugene 97401; (541) 682-7888
eugenesciencecenter.org

Anyone young at heart will enjoy learning with this center's multitude of hands-on activities. From the Discovery Room and its fossils, bones, and rocks and minerals, to the high-tech planetarium, this center strives to inspire children and adults to love science. Start by catching a show at the planetarium, and then head into the main hall and its interactive exhibits. The exhibits on display vary, but they usually highlight astronomy, engineering, and optics. If you're visiting with young children, check out the Tot Spot for activities perfect for the younger set. Whether you are gazing at fossils and meteorites, or peering at the stars in the planetarium, the Eugene Science Center is a family-friendly escape any time of year.

2 Hatfield Marine Science Visitor Center

2030 SE Marine Science Drive, Newport 97365; (541) 867-0100
seagrant.oregonstate.edu/visitor-center

When you enter this center focused on marine science, you'll be greeted by two octopuses: the first is part of a large mural on the exterior windows; the other is a real eight-tentacled wonder you can observe in her tank or online via the site's OctoCam. In addition, the site offers touch tanks with starfish, fish, and even anemones. There's also a tsunami wave tank where visitors can build a LEGO house to see if it survives a simulated tsunami, a hands-on tank about erosion, and an augmented-reality sandbox. If you time your visit right (check the website). you can even watch the octopus eat her lunch. Once you're done, the center is located quite close to hiking trails, as well as some wonderful scenic views of Yaquina Bay (see page 48).

3 Lava Lands Visitor Center

58201 S. US 97, Bend 97707; (541) 593-2421
tinyurl.com/lavalandsvisitorcenter

Open from May through the first week of October (check the website for specific dates and times), Lava Lands gets its name from the stark, black, barren rock—long-cooled lava—that erupted from Lava

Butte around 7,000 years ago. The site includes a number of nearby hiking paths through the eerie, surreal landscape, and the visitor center features films, ranger-led talks, and more. In the summer, the visitor center also offers an affordable shuttle (check for schedule) that'll take you to the summit of Lava Butte and its panoramic views. If you think the site looks like the surface of the moon, you're not alone: NASA astronauts trained in the area in preparation for the Apollo moon landings.

4 Oregon Museum of Science and Industry

1945 SE Water Ave., Portland 97214; (503) 797-4000
omsi.edu

With five exhibit halls, 200 interactive exhibits, a planetarium, and a restored submarine (the USS *Blueback)* moored on-site in the Willamette River, the Oregon Museum of Science and Industry has enough to hold your interest for days. The museum also hosts traveling exhibits and is home to six themed labs that all ages will enjoy. When you get hungry, stop in for a snack at the cafe or a meal at the Theory Restaurant or the Empirical Cafe. However you venture through this museum, stop by the Science Store on your way out for some take-home fun.

5 ScienceWorks

1500 E. Main St., Ashland 97520; (541) 482-6767
scienceworksmuseum.org

Known as the hands-on museum, ScienceWorks boasts a medley of interactive exhibits to help kids and families explore the wonders of science. With live science demonstrations and long-standing favorites such as DaVinci's Garage, and Discovery Island, a large space dedicated to children 5 and younger, there are options to educate and entertain those of any age. The museum's showcase exhibits change over time (recent ones have focused on the physics of flight, and the 50th anniversary of the Apollo 11 landing), so there is always a fresh reason to plan a visit.

6 Sunriver Nature Center & Observatory

57245 River Road, Sunriver 97707; (541) 593-4394
snco.org

Perfect for a visit day or night, this wonderful site is located alongside Lake Aspen and preserves 8 acres of land with trails for hiking, biking, and wildlife-watching. At night, it's a stargazing destination. Home to clear, dark skies and an observatory that has more than a dozen telescopes, which are often pre-focused on specific targets in the night sky, making it an easy way to introduce kids and beginners to the wonders of the heavens. The observatory's astronomers also lead guided star talks and constellation tours, helping you put a name to the star patterns whirling overhead.

The upper Multnomah Falls

OREGON IS HOME to hundreds of waterfalls, and waterfall hikes (and photography) are practically a pastime in the state. The waterfalls included here are simply a sampler, and they range from the towering Multnomah Falls, outside Portland, to the diminutive but striking Hug Point Falls, accessible only at low tide.

Note: When hiking near waterfalls, keep your surroundings, road conditions, tides, and safety in mind. Optimal waterfall-viewing usually depends on the season and weather—a waterfall that's in full flow during the spring may slow to a trickle at other times of year—so check conditions before you go.

WATERFALLS

Waterfalls

 Statewide

1 Columbia Gorge Waterfalls

Statewide
fs.usda.gov/recmain/crgnsa/recreation

A massive canyon spanning dozens of miles on the Columbia River, the Columbia Gorge contains dozens of different waterfalls, including plunges, cascades, falls with multiple drops, and more. Because there is so much to see, there are many ways to explore it. To plan your trip, visit the website for the Columbia River Gorge National Scenic Area (listed above). The gorge's steep canyon walls formed during the Missoula Floods, when a massive glacial lake scoured out the valleys, leaving behind bare rock and numerous waterfalls. Plan your waterfall hikes based on your ambition and needs: some are ADA accessible, while others are not, and it's easy to string together several fall visits into the same trip. A few notable waterfalls in the Gorge include two-tiered Bridal Veil Falls (in the town of Bridal Veil), with a 118-foot drop and Tunnel Falls (accessible via the Eagle Creek Trailhead), where a tunnel was blasted out behind the falls (though traversing the tunnel can be dangerous, so use caution).

2 Drift Creek Falls

Siuslaw National Forest Forest Service Road 18, east of Lincoln City; (503) 392-5100
tinyurl.com/driftcreekfallsoregon

Located about 16 miles east of Lincoln City, at this trailhead you can walk through a slice of Siuslaw National Forest on an easy 1.5-mile path (3 miles round-trip). From the trailhead (see the link above for directions and a brochure), you'll head downhill, crossing two little wooden bridges that bring you over a stream that continues with your stroll. As you keep descending, you'll start to hear the waterfall, and you'll cross another footbridge, where you'll see a big suspension bridge. Continue on the main trail and you'll arrive at a steel suspension bridge and the falls cascading down. From here, you can walk across the suspension bridge and continue to the end of the trail, or you can return to your starting point.

3 Hug Point Falls

Hug Point State Recreation Site Oregon Coast Highway, Arch Cape 97102;
(503) 368-3575
tinyurl.com/hugpoint

The falls at this scenic site are only 25 feet wide with a 15-foot drop (and they're only present with adequate rainfall), but the surrounding scenery is what makes it worth a visit. Accessible only at low tide—be sure to consult a tide table before you visit—it's just a short walk north from the parking area to the Pacific Ocean and Hug Point Falls. As the water gently streams over the rock, the ocean scoops it back up. There are also sea caves to explore, and Cannon Beach's famous Haystack Rock is just about 5 miles up the road. Hug Point gets its name because stagecoaches once had to stay close to the point, even at low tide.

Note: This area is accessible only at low tide. If in doubt, don't venture out.

4 Multnomah Falls

Multnomah Lodge 48314 E. Historic Columbia River Highway, Corbett 97010;
(503) 695-2372, (541) 308-1700
tinyurl.com/multnomahfallsoregon

Featuring two drops that combine for a height of 620 feet, this is the most-visited—and tallest—waterfall in the Columbia Gorge (and the entire state). Multnomah's waters tumble down Larch Mountain, exposing several successive basalt flows. Open year-round, winter and spring are the ideal times to visit the falls, but, in the height of tourist season, expect a crowd. The falls draw more than 2 million visitors a year. An ADA-accessible hike from the parking area takes you to one of the best places for pictures: Benson Bridge, which sits directly in front of the roaring water. Those wanting a tougher hike can continue up another 2.4 miles (not accessible). After you're done, stop by Multnomah Lodge (the address we're directing you to here) to grab some hot chocolate or lunch at the restaurant on your way out.

5 Munson Creek Falls

Munson Creek Falls State Natural Site Munson Creek Road, Tillamook 97141;
(503) 842-3182
tinyurl.com/munsoncreekfalls

Nestled amid the Coast Range, at 319 feet this is the tallest waterfall in these mountains. The walk to this beauty is a little more than a half mile on a flat path. You'll walk along a small stream with moss-covered trees lying across it. The rushing sound of water comes before the falls

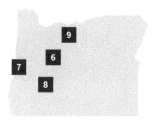

that slowly becomes visible from the forest. As you walk, you may notice the red cedar trees, not just because they are towering, but also for their smell that drifts in. All of this makes the area a feast for the senses. Though you can visit at any time, winter is great, as the coastal rains will fill the falls. Winter is also salmon spawning season, so sit back and watch the roaring falls and see if you can spot salmon in the water.

6 Sahalie and Koosah Falls

Willamette National Forest OR 126 near milepost 5, McKenzie Bridge 97413; (541) 822-3381
tinyurl.com/sahalieandkoosahfalls

Sahalie and Koosah Falls are both accessible via a loop trail (see link above for map). You can start at the parking areas for either falls. From there, venture along the path to take in bird-watching and squirrel spotting until you reach the next waterfall. Sahalie features water cascading down 100 feet down; Koosah Falls is slightly smaller at "only" 70 feet tall, with the water dropping into a deep pool.

7 Sweet Creek Falls

Siuslaw National Forest Sweet Creek Road, Mapleton 97453; (541) 750-7000; tinyurl.com/sweetcreekfallstrail

Located just over 10 miles south of Mapleton on Sweet Creek Road, Sweet Creek boasts 11 waterfalls and four separate trail sections for a total of about 2.2 miles (round-trip). Starting from the Homestead Trailhead (see above link for directions), you will find yourself on a rutted road with portions that were created by wooden wagons. A common favorite is a gentle four-tiered waterfall best described as meditative. If you visit on a hot day, there are several places where you can stick your feet into the shallows.

8 Watson Falls

Umpqua Falls National Forest Fish Creek Road (Forest Service Road 37), Roseburg 97471; (541) 957-3200
tinyurl.com/watsonfalls

Located in Umpqua National Forest and suffused with greenery, wildflowers (in season), and with dark basalt underfoot, the setting for Watson Falls couldn't be more idyllic. Then there is the waterfall, an impressive 272 feet tall and the tallest in southwest Oregon. The hike from the Watson Falls Trailhead is only about a half-mile long. The best view is at the end from a wooden bridge that lets you take in just how tall and majestic this waterfall is. Picnic tables are nearby, so pack a lunch and enjoy the experience as long as you want.

9 White River Falls

White River Falls State Park Near The Dalles; GPS: 45.24166, -121.09444;
(800) 551-6949
tinyurl.com/whiteriverfallsoregon

Open seasonally, this park is well-known for the remains of a power plant that is tucked beneath a towering waterfall. In 1910, a hydroelectric power plant was built here to harness the power of the 90-foot, two-tier falls that produced electricity until 1963. The abandoned hydroelectric plant still sits on the canyon floor. A relatively short 1.4-mile hike leads to expansive views and surviving portions of the power plant. But be advised that the hike can be rugged, especially if you stray off trail. Along the hike you'll see Devils Halfacre, a forbidding but beautifully austere landscape in the distance. You'll also get a view of Celestial Falls (the lower tier of the falls). Eventually, after a catwalk and some uneven steps, you'll reach the power plant itself. While it's now rusted over, you can still steal glances inside the old buildings.

Note: The water here may look tranquil, but it can be dangerous. It's recommended that you stay out of it.

Koosah Falls on the MacKenzie River

Mt. Bachelor skiing

WITH ITS MOUNTAINS covered in snow through the winter and well into spring, Oregon is a destination for skiers, snowboarders, snowmobilers, and other snow lovers. Better yet, some of the best destinations for snow sports are near the state's biggest cities, making them relatively accessible. If you want a remote escape for winter fun, that's an option too!

Note: Many of the following sites require admission or a Sno-Park permit (see tinyurl.com/oregonsnoparkpermits). Be sure to visit the site for driving directions—seasonal road closures are common in some parts of mountain country, not to mention that GPS or online mapping programs may not be accurate.

SNOW

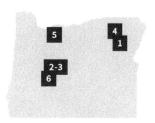

1 Anthony Lakes Mountain Resort

47500 Anthony Lakes Highway, North Powder 97867; (541) 856-3277;
anthonylakes.com

Nestled in the Elkhorn Mountains, Anthony Lakes Mountain Resort features 21 ski runs and 30 kilometers of groomed Nordic trails; the trails vary in difficulty, and there's a healthy sampling of intermediate-to-expert-level trails and ski runs, but beginners shouldn't fret, as there are plenty of options for newbies too. And you can expect snow! Anthony Lakes receives around 300 inches—25 feet!—of snow each year. If you really want to find fresh powder and go on an adventure, you can rent a seat in a snowcat adventure (though make your reservations online well in advance). The resort also has a few lodging options on-site (including heated yurts) or lodging partners in the area. The resort serves food and drinks in its lodge and saloon.

2 Elk Lake Resort

60000 Century Drive, Bend 97701; (541) 480-7378
elklakeresort.net

Accessible in winter only by snowcat or snowmobile, the remoteness of this resort is part of the allure. Elk Lake is surrounded by national forests and wilderness areas, and it's known as a snowmobiling destination. Snowshoers, fat-tire bikers, and cross-country skiing fans will find much to enjoy as well. There are several lodging options in the winter, ranging from fully furnished cabins with kitchens to more bare-bones camper cabins with heat but no power. If you're hungry the on-site restaurant offers fresh, tasty foods and drinks.

3 Mt. Bachelor

13000 SW Century Drive, Bend 97702; (541) 382-1709
mtbachelor.com

Topping out at more than 9,000 feet, Mt. Bachelor is an imposing sight. It is also home to one of North America's largest ski resorts. With more than 4,300 acres and 100 ski runs in all, it has everything from double black diamonds to hills more suited for beginners, or those who've never strapped on a pair of skis at all. While the focus may be skiing and snowboarding, there is plenty of space for any snow enthusiast. The site offers snowshoeing tours, tubing, ranger-led ski tours, and even dog sled rides with a professional musher. Mt. Bachelor's Woodward Mountain Park offers areas dedicated for all ability levels, including the youngest. The Woodward Start Park is free and is designed as a "playground on snow" to introduce the newest skiers and riders to show sports.

4 Mt. Emily Recreation Park

Umatilla National Forest Forest Service Road 31, 19 miles west of La Grande; (541) 278-3716
tinyurl.com/mtemilysnopark

Cross-country ski or snowshoe amid stunning views of Meacham Canyon. Seated in the Blue Mountains, Mt. Emily Sno-Park (also known as the Meacham Divide) has a stunning setting as well as 18 miles of volunteer-groomed cross-country trails. The trails are all 12 feet wide, and they are usually in use from early winter into March (depending on weather and snow). With creative names like Butcher and Roller Coaster, there are some challenging trails, but there are also some, such as the Loppet Trail, that are more suitable for beginners. And don't miss Loppet Point, which features a spectacular view.

5 Mt. Hood SkiBowl

87000 US 26, Government Camp 97028; (503) 272-3206
kibowl.com

Located on Mt. Hood, the SkiBowl features an almost dizzying array of options for winter fun. It features 65 ski runs, with options for all skill levels, and it includes more than 30 runs with lights for night skiing. In addition, there's an adventure park for tubing on-site, terrain parks for snowboarders, a tubing carousel, snowmobiles for kids, and even a two-story indoor Super Play Zone for younger kids.

6 Salt Creek Sno-Park

Willamette National Forest OR 58 (Willamette Highway) at milepost 57, Oakridge 97463; (541) 782-2283
tinyurl.com/saltcreeksnopark

Salt Creek Sno-Park is home to a number of rather different options for wintertime fun. The site's Snow Play area is perfect for sledding and tubing; you can snowshoe or ski the Salt Creek Falls Trail to see Salt Creek Falls, the state's second-tallest waterfall, frozen in place. The really adventurous can connect with the nearby Island and Birthday Lake trail system, which leads to a strenuous uphill trip, and eventually the backcountry Fuji Shelter that offers a spot to warm up and even a loft where you can stay the night. (See the U.S. Forest Service website above for details.)

7 Virginia Meissner Sno-Park

Cascade Lakes Highway 14 miles west of Bend; (541) 316-0831;
meissnernordic.org

Enthusiasts of cross-country skiing and snowshoeing will want to
visit this Sno-Park situated amid the Cascade Mountains. It features
20 groomed trails, with another 5 ungroomed options. The trails
vary in length from just under a half mile to treks like the Tangent
Loop that cover 5.5 miles. In all, the park has more than 40 kilometers of cross-country trails to explore. The site also occasionally hosts
special events, such as races, and even a luminaria: a special night
where skiers and snowshoers are guided along the trail by candlelight If you happen to get a bit chilled on your visit, warm up in the
lodge by the trailhead.

Mt. Hood in all its snowy glory

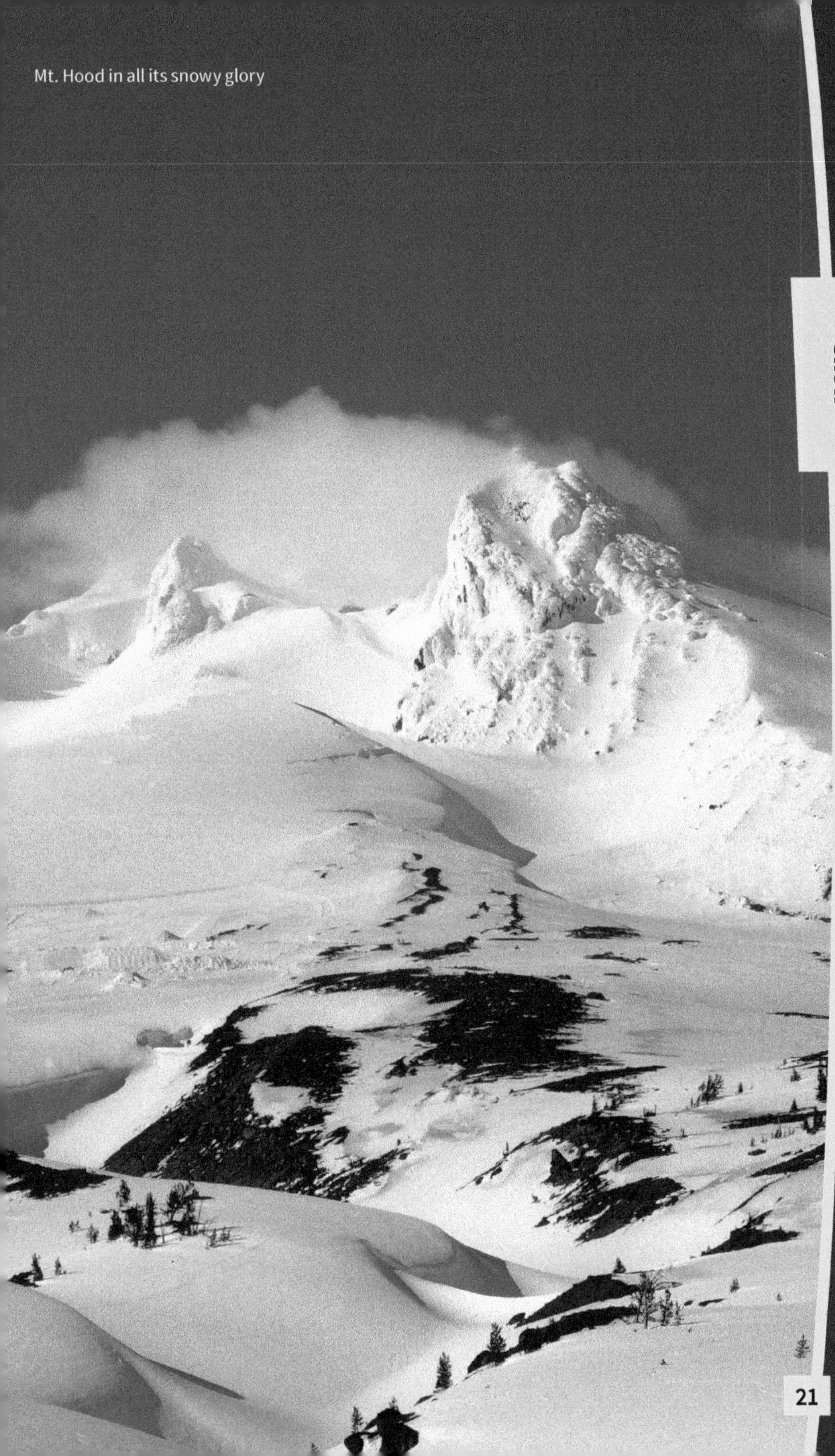

A B-25 Mitchell Bomber at the Evergreen Aviation Museum

WHETHER YOU WANT to see vintage fighter jets, check out an SR-71 Blackbird spy plane, or take a flight to do some sightseeing, Oregon is a great place for aviation buffs to visit.

AIRPLANES & AVIATION

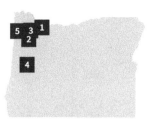

1 Envi Adventures

1350 NW Perimeter Way, Troutdale 97060; (855) 236-8466
enviadventures.com

When you book a tour with Envi Adventures, you've got options. Perhaps you want to see Portland from the air on the Stumptown tour, or perhaps a waterfall tour is more your thing. Soar over Mount Hood and Sandy River to view quicksand from the only safe angle. If you want a longer tour, you can fly past Mount Hood and its adjacent national forest. If you think Oregon's wonders are gorgeous from the ground, just wait until you see them from the air.

2 Evergreen Aviation and Space Museum

500 NE Captain Michael King Smith Way, McMinnville 97128; (503) 434-4180
evergreenmuseum.org

During World War II, metal was rationed for military use, and Liberty ships bringing arms and supplies to Europe were hunted by German submarines. Henry Kaiser was the most prominent ship builder of his day and knew all too well how perilous life in Liberty ships could be. He suggested that a lightweight but massive airplane could counter the submarine threat. Famed airplane developer Howard Hughes soon took on the job, and he crafted the *Spruce Goose* almost entirely out of birch (despite its nickname). In the end, its wingspan was 320 feet long; it took to the skies once, flying for about a mile. The historic airplane is one of the many highlights at this museum, which offers tours of the famous plane. This museum is also home to an SR-71 Blackbird (the world's fastest air-breathing plane); helicopters; and an entire building dedicated to the history of space exploration, with rocket engines, replicas of the Apollo command module and lunar module, and even a replica lunar rover. The museum also has a flight simulator; cafés; and movies about space flight, aviation, and the military.

3 Jetliner Home in the Woods

15270 SW Holly Hill Road, Hillsboro 97123
airplanehome.com

More than a decade ago, Bruce Campbell turned a retired Boeing 727 into a 1,066-square-foot home. Nestled in the Oregon forest, this lovingly preserved jetliner is now Campbell's residence, and not only does he graciously welcome visitors, he occasionally allows guests to spend the night. For visiting hours, house rules, and safety warnings, and to learn about all the planning that went into creating this one-of-a-kind Oregon home, visit the website above. The plane itself is occasionally used as a space for concerts; check concertonawing.com for more information. If you're keen to build your own aviation-inspired home in the woods, Campbell offers much hard-won wisdom on his website.

4 Oregon Air and Space Museum

90377 Boeing Drive, Eugene 97402; (541) 461-1101
oasmuseum.com

Located right next to the Eugene airport, this museum is dedicated to preserving aviation and space flight history. The museum houses several different aircraft, including fighters such as the Russian-made MIG-17, attack planes like the A-4 Skyhawk, and smaller propeller-driven planes. The museum also has exhibits dedicated to Oregon's flying aces, model planes, commercial airlines, and historic military uniforms. Visiting hours at the museum are relatively limited, so be sure to check ahead before heading out.

5 Tillamook Air Museum

6030 Hangar Road, Tillamook; (503) 842-1130
tillamookair.com

This museum occupies the site of the former Tillamook Naval Air Station. In 1942, the Navy built two wooden hangars here to house Navy airships, which were used to patrol the coasts and spot enemy submarines. One of the hangars still survives, and today it houses the Tillamook Air Museum. The museum houses a wide variety of aircraft, from the F-14s made famous by *Top Gun* to home-built projects, helicopters, and a number of fire trucks and other vehicles. The site is also home to a locomotive built in 1917, exhibits pertaining to World War II–era aircraft, and life during the war. The museum is currently restoring the fuselage of a Convair 880 jetliner. The site has a family-friendly Kids Korner where can kids can play on kid-size wooden versions of a biplane, a boat, and a locomotive.

An idyllic scene at the Portland Japanese Garden

WHETHER YOU WANT to see the roses that give Portland its nickname (Rose City), rainforests on the coast with towering trees and ferns, or the cherry blossoms of a Japanese garden, Oregon is replete with gardens and green spaces.

Note: The International Rose Test Garden, Hoyt Arboretum, and Portland Japanese Garden are all part of Washington Park (explorewashingtonpark.org).

GARDENS

Gardens

1 Crystal Springs Rhododendron Garden

5801 SE 28th Ave., Portland 97202; (503) 771-8386
tinyurl.com/crystalspringsportland

Before this was a garden, it was a farm, but rhododendrons have grown here for more than a century; the oldest rhododendron here was planted before 1917. The garden opened in 1950 and received current name in 1964. Today, the garden has a number of features, including waterfalls crafted from rocks taken from Mt. Hood and Mt. Adams. The main draw, of course, is a bounty of rhododendrons, azaleas, and other plants along its paved and unpaved paths. Ideal to visit any time of year, the garden is open year-round. The park is well-known for its annual plant sales, including a Mother's Day Show, an Early Show, and others. When you visit, be on the lookout for more than blooms: this is also a bird-watching hot spot, with nearly 100 species spotted in the park.

2 Hoyt Arboretum

4000 SW Fairview Blvd., Portland 97221; (503) 865-8733
hoytarboretum.org

Covering 190 acres in all, Hoyt Arboretum is home to 2,300 species of trees and plants from around the world. It also has 12 miles of trails, including some that are ADA accessible. Start at the visitor center, where you'll find trail maps and brochures, as well as information about guided tours (in season), classes and activities, and programming options for kids and families. One fun kid-friendly program is Tree Time, a guided hands-on look at nature, plants, and insects for kids ages 2–4. Given the sheer diversity of plants on-site, there's almost always something gorgeous to enjoy!

3 International Rose Test Garden

4033 SW Canyon Road, Portland 97221; (503) 319-0999
tinyurl.com/rosetestgarden

At the height of World War I, Jesse Currey, a Portland gardener and newspaper editor, urged the city to establish a garden to serve as a safe haven for rose varieties from Europe that were potentially in danger. The war ended, but the plans for the garden went on, and it's still around today, with more than 10,000 rose bushes and 600 different varieties (with a handful of new varieties replaced each year). There are actually several gardens here in all. A favorite is the Shakespeare Garden; it was originally intended to include all of the plants mentioned in Shakespeare's plays, but it now features roses named after Shakespearean characters. Guided tours of the garden are also available, as is a gift shop with all sorts of items and products related to roses.

4 Lan Su Chinese Garden

239 NW Everett St., Portland 97209; (503) 228-8131
lansugarden.org

Portland's sister city is Suzhou, a Chinese city in Jiangsu province, which is known for its famous Ming Dynasty architecture and garden. In the year 2000, the two cities collaborated on the construction of the Lan Su garden, with Chinese builders and craftspeople visiting to design and construct the garden, making it a truly authentic and unique place to visit. The garden offers wonderful greenery and scenery at any time of year, and don't miss the seasonal plant guides they offer. In addition to the beautiful architecture, it's also a great place to introduce yourself to wider Chinese culture, as it hosts demonstrations of folk art, lantern-lighting ceremonies at the Chinese New Year, and even Chinese conversation classes.

5 The Oregon Garden

879 W. Main St., Silverton 97381; (503) 874-8100
oregongarden.org

The Oregon Garden is more than just one garden; it has more than 20 themed gardens to enjoy. If you're looking for a serene, quiet walk, visit the Bosque Garden. In Spanish, the word Bosque means "grove" and it's a fitting name for this garden's reflecting ponds and maple trees, each of which have their own planter boxes. The Children's Garden has a treehouse, a real underground Hobbit house, and a dinosaur dig. There's also a rose garden, a medicinal garden, a Northwest garden with regional plants, a sensory garden full of rich scents and textures, and many others. The garden's Oak Grove even has a 400-year-old oak tree. Because there is so much to see here, it's worth making several trips; if you want to see as much as possible, there's a tram (open April–October) that winds just under 1.5 miles through the garden. The tram trip lasts 25 minutes, and there are six stops where you can exit or enter. If you want to stay on-site, you can stay at the lovely Oregon Garden Resort; also, when you visit, don't miss the nearby Frank Lloyd Wright Gordon House, the only structure designed by Wright in the Pacific Northwest (thegordonhouse.org).

Portland Japanese Garden

611 SW Kingston Ave., Portland 97205; (503) 223-1321
japanesegarden.org

Built not long after the end of World War II, in the spirit of reconciliation between the U.S. and Japan, this beautiful space features five distinct Japanese gardens, as well as a cultural village with an arts center dedicated to introducing visitors to Japanese culture and art. The gardens range from the serene Flat Garden and its raked gravel to the spacious Strolling Pond Garden with its connected ponds. Garden tours are available, as are cultural demonstrations or performances of traditional Japanese arts and crafts. Don't miss the on-site café, offering authentic Japanese tea, or the gift shop and its Japanese wares; check the website periodically, as the garden also hosts special traveling exhibitions.

7 Prehistoric Gardens

36848 US 101 S., Port Orford 97465; (541) 332-4463
prehistoricgardens.com

Watch out or the triceratops on the trail may catch you off-guard. Though the three-block walk around this temperate rainforest is short, the fun is in the quirky roadside statues of 23 dinosaurs and other prehistoric animals and informative plaques. Kids will enjoy the dinos and scrambling over one of the five wooden bridges and the gravel path is both wheelchair and stroller accessible. The garden also winds through a temperate rainforest with some truly impressive vegetation and trees. An on-site gift shop sells keepsakes.

8 Shore Acres State Park

Cape Arago Highway, Coos Bay 97420; (541) 888-3732
tinyurl.com/shoreacresstatepark

Once the oceanfront estate of timber heir and developer Louis Simpson, this state park has something of an unhappy past. Simpson built the house in 1906 and lived there with his wife, Cassandra, starting in 1915. (He named the mansion Shoreacres, but she preferred it spelled as two words.) Sadly, however, Simpson's fortunes soon changed: in 1918 he campaigned unsuccessfully to

Gardens

be the Republican nominee for governor of Oregon; then, in 1921, his wife died, and his mansion burned down that same year. Simpson remarried and lived in a surviving home on the estate, but the Great Depression eventually sank Simpson's finances. The State of Oregon took over the property, and today it's known for both its breathtaking seaside views (several of Simpson's properties are now state parks) and its immaculate gardens. The park is home to a formal garden, a Japanese garden, rose gardens, and, during the holiday season, wonderful light displays. After you take in the gardens, head to the observation building, where you can get a weatherproof look at the dramatic seas below and see panels about the long-gone mansion. You might even spot whales in the distance.

The International Rose Test Garden in Portland

Crater Lake, a wonder to behold

OREGON IS PART of the famous (or infamous) Pacific Rim of Fire, an area where tectonic and volcanic activity have dramatically shaped the landscape and habitats for millions of years. But Oregon's story is more than just one of earthquakes, lava, and volcanoes: Oregon also has scenic vistas reminiscent of the Southwest, picturesque volcanic lakes, and sedimentary rocks that preserve a variety of fascinating fossils.

Note: Some of the sites in this section are in relatively remote parts of Oregon, are closed seasonally due to weather or to protect rare species, or could prove hazardous if you're not prepared for the conditions you find. So use this section to read up and get inspired—then do your homework before you go.

GEOLOGY & PALEONTOLOGY

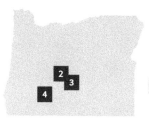

1 Various locations

1 Agate Hunting and Beachcombing

Along the Oregon coast, but especially Newport
Collecting rules: oregondiscovery.com/rockhounding-regulations

Beachcombing is a popular pastime across much of the Oregon coast and beyond, and it's a treat in large part because you never know what you'll find. Agates are popular; these hard, translucent stones with well-defined bands are often found on Oregon beaches. Specimens are often small (marble-size to golf ball–size) but occasionally run larger. They range in color from clear to red and rarely even blue. For a good introduction to agates, as well as their lookalikes, pick up *Agates and Other Collectibles of the Pacific Coast* by Dan Lynch. Agates aren't the only interesting finds; jasper and other beach stones are fun keepsakes, as are small pieces of driftwood.

Keep in mind that there are collecting limits for agates in Oregon: you can collect a gallon per person, per day, with a limit of 3 gallons a year. You can collect 5 gallons of cobble per day and 10 gallons per year. For driftwood, you can collect no more than a cubic yard (3 feet by 3 feet by 3 feet) per day and three cords per year. *Note:* Happily, all beaches in Oregon are open to the public (and collecting) thanks to the popular "Beach Bill" signed into law in 1967.

2 Big Obsidian Flow

Newberry National Volcanic Monument, Deschutes National Forest
Forest Service Road 21, about 25 miles south of Bend; GPS: 43.70680, -121.23660; (541) 593-2421
tinyurl.com/bigobsidianflow

Open seasonally (call ahead to ensure it's open), this is one of those sites that rockhounds and fans of volcanology *have* to see. On this 1-mile remote trail, you'll see where a very young (geologically speaking) lava flow hardened quickly into a mix of pumice and black obsidian (volcanic glass). There are stairs on the walk, and you'll definitely want sturdy shoes, as the glass can be quite sharp. For the same reason, this trip isn't well suited for dogs. Also, during the height of the summer season it can get really warm on this hike, so make sure you bring water, sunscreen, and the like. But the effort getting here is worth it, as it's a surreal, serene environment.

One last note: Collecting obsidian here is strictly illegal, so please take only pictures.

3 Crack-in-the-Ground

Crack-in-the-Ground Road, about 7 miles north of Christmas Valley; GPS: 43.33281, -120.67600; (541) 947-2177; blm.gov/visit/crack-ground

Crack-in-the-Ground is a perfectly good description for this site, where a volcanic fissure created a long, thin, canyon-like depression in the ground tens of thousands of years ago. More often than not, such features fill in quickly with water and sediment. Crack-in-the-Ground, however, never filled in, as the area where it formed is arid. In all, the fissure runs for more than 2 miles, and it reaches up to 70 feet deep. If you visit, there's a hiking path open year-round that covers about 2 miles, but dress warm, as it's often much colder at the bottom of the canyon (up to 20°F or so). Also, before you head out, be sure to check the Bureau of Land Management website above for directions and conditions, and head out in a vehicle that can handle the trip—four-wheel drive is definitely recommended.

4 Crater Lake National Park

OR 62, Crater Lake 97604; (541) 594-3000
nps.gov/crla

This famous lake formed around 7,500 years ago when a volcano erupted and its crater collapsed. The crater filled in with water, creating this staggeringly gorgeous and incredibly deep lake (1,943 feet at its deepest point). Now preserved as a national park, it's open year-round, though check ahead on travel conditions/road closures if you visit when the snow could fly. If you think the lake's bright blue is exceptional, it is! It's some of the purest water on the planet, and there are plenty of ways to enjoy the park. Hiking and walking are popular options, and so is driving on Scenic Rim Drive, which encircles the crater and has more than two dozen overlooks. If you want to get on the water, private watercraft (including kayaks, canoes, and the like) are not allowed due to the possibility of introducing invasive species, but you can book a seat on a charter boat that travels out on the lake, and even one that brings you to Wizard Island, the volcano's cinder cone.

Note: The volcano has been dormant for some time, but it's not extinct, so heed any park warnings or closures that may arise. Also, getting to the boat dock requires a steep hike that's about a 2-mile round-trip, so plan accordingly.

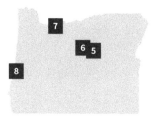

5 John Day Fossil Beds National Monument

32651 OR 19, Kimberly 97848; (541) 987-2333
nps.gov/joda

In 1812, while working for the Pacific Fur Company, John Day and a partner were robbed—even their clothing was taken—where the Mah-Hah River meets the Columbia. They were later rescued, but travelers often pointed out the spot where he was robbed, and the river was later re-named after him. John Day himself never found a fossil, but the river where he was robbed is home to some of the finest fossil beds in the country. The fossils here range in age from around 44 million years old—when this part of Oregon had a warm, wet climate and wildly diverse plant and animal life—to just 7 million years ago, when the landscape looked a lot more familiar, but the resident wildlife found then was still pretty amazing: rhinos, saber-toothed cats, even long-gone bear species. Today, there are three park units in all: Clarno, Painted Hills, and Sheep Rock. Consider starting at Sheep Rock; the address listed above will bring you to the Thomas Condon Paleontology Visitor Center, where you can learn all about the fossil beds, see displays, and even take a gander at a pale-ontology lab with real fossil excavation in the works. There are also hiking trails nearby where you can see fossils in the ground, though collecting is strictly forbidden. Also check out the historic Cant Ranch and Home (staffed only in the summer). If you want to visit the Painted Hills, one of the park's other units, see the next profile.

6 John Day Fossil Beds National Monument, Painted Hills Unit

Bear Creek Road, about 9 miles northwest of Mitchell (about halfway between Portland and Boise, Idaho); (541) 987-2333;
nps.gov/joda/planyourvisit/ptd-hills-unit.htm

A separate unit of the John Day Fossil Beds National Monument (see previous profile), the Painted Hills are an Oregon wonder. The colorful striped rocks here are worth a visit in spring, summer, or fall, as the views and shadows change with the available light and moisture levels. These hills formed over millions of years, as the mineral

Geology & Paleontology

36

content of the river plain changed over time. The color bands in the hills correspond to different minerals that were deposited by the river. The park recommends viewing the hills in the afternoon, as it offers the best light for photos. This is also a destination in spring, when wildflowers pop up, making for a stunning contrast with the hills in the background. When you visit, there are also several relatively brief hiking trails (0.25–1.6 miles round-trip) to check out. The Carroll Rim Trail leads to a panoramic view, and the Painted Overlook Trail leads to a scenic overlook. Other trails provide access to distinct views of the hills or introduce you to this section's fossil history. Whichever adventure you choose, please stay on the trails—this will preserve the area's scenic beauty and protect its wildlife.

7 Lost Lake

Willamette National Forest   Just north of US 20/OR 126, 30 miles from McKenzie Bridge; GPS: 44.42927, -121.91247; (541) 822-3381
tinyurl.com/lostlakeor

This lake is something of a contradiction: when the water levels are high, it's a popular catch-and-release fishing spot, but when water levels are low, the lake drains away, leaving behind soggy marshland, and sometimes an entirely dry lakebed. The water drains from one or more holes, and when the water level is low, you can see these "drains." The precise cause of the now-you-see-it, now-you-don't lake isn't entirely understood, but it's definitely tied to the region's volcanic history, and the water almost certainly drains to an underground river and eventually to another water body. In this respect, the lake is sort of like a bathtub with an open drain: the lake "fills up" again when the water level coming into the lake from streams and rain is greater than the amount siphoned off by the drain.

Note: Please don't get too close to the drain, as it may be unstable, and be careful if there's a lot of water moving into it, for obvious reasons. It makes for great pictures from a safe distance, however.

8 Oregon Dunes National Recreation Area

Visitor Center   855 US 101, Reedsport 97467; (541) 271-6000;
tinyurl.com/oregondunesnra

The dunes you'll find in this recreation area, which is part of Siuslaw National Forest and covers 40 miles from Coos Bay to Florence, are the result of an ancient mountain range that was worn down over millions of years. The resulting sand was swept into rivers, reaching the sea, and it eventually was pushed onto shore through a combination of wave action, wind, and tides. The end result is a unique—and massive—natural wonderland that is now popular for everything from sandboarding and hiking to camping and off-highway-vehicle riding (in select areas). It's even more surreal because of the juxtaposition between forest, ocean, and sand seen in many portions of the recreation area.

Sandboarding is exactly what it sounds like—using a specialized board to slide down on the sand. Boards are available for rent at many places along the coast. But before you head out, keep the season in mind, as certain dunes and beaches are closed because the dunes are a specialized habitat for the threatened western snowy plover. Off-highway vehicles (for example, dune buggies and all-terrain vehicles) are allowed in a handful of areas of the dunes, and rentals are available along the coast, but to stay safe (and legal—noise limits are enforced), make sure you do your homework ahead of time. However you enjoy the dunes, it's an incredible place to visit, so don't miss it.

9 Thor's Well

Cape Perpetua Visitor Center 2400 US 101, Yachats 97498; (541) 547-3289; tinyurl.com/thorswellcapeperpetua

Imagine Thor's Hammer smashing into the Pacific, crushing the seafloor and causing water to explode into the air. Located a short (0.8 mile round-trip) hike from the Cape Perpetua Visitor Center (the address listed above), at high tide Thor's Hammer is famous for its "bowl" of water that fills from below, then bursts into an impressive spray. Likely a collapsed sea cave, Thor's Hammer constantly fills and refills at high tide, but at low tide, you can see the empty "bowl." If you visit, make sure to check the tides beforehand, and also be on the lookout for "sneaker waves," powerful waves that appear without warning and can knock you down when you don't expect it. Always keep an eye on the ocean, or simply view Thor's Hammer from a distance.

The John Day Fossil Beds and its painted hills

Oregon Caves National Monument and Preserve

OREGON HAS MORE CAVES than you'd think, but they are often located in remote, far-flung areas that are hard to access or they're closed entirely due to wildlife, paleontological sites, or safety reasons. With that said, there are some wonderful caves (or cave-like features) that are open to the public seasonally.

Note: When visiting a cave, always dress warmly bring multiple light sources, wear solid footwear, and stay away from wildlife, such as bats or snakes. Also, if you've gone caving elsewhere, don't rewear or reuse any of the same gear, clothes, or shoes to prevent the spread of the fungus that leads to white-nose syndrome, a disease that is fatal in bats.

CAVES

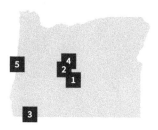

1 Derrick Cave

Near Fort Rock; GPS: 43.52043, -120.86400; (541) 947-2177
blm.gov/visit/derrick-cave

The road to get to this cave is part of the adventure—it's about 23 miles northeast of Fort Rock, but the drive there is quite rough (see the link above for a map, but note that it's best to call for directions beforehand), so it'll take some careful planning (and a suitable vehicle) to get there. Once you get there, the cave is a beauty. About a quarter of a mile long, 50 feet wide, and 30 feet high, you have to scramble into it, but it's neat, and the skylights (openings in the roof) often make for pretty photographs. When you visit, be sure to dress warmly, as the cave is quite chilly.

The cave also has a somewhat disquieting place in history; during the height of the Cold War, the cave was designated as a fallout shelter and stocked with emergency supplies, which are long since gone.

2 Lava River Cave

Deschutes National Forest   Cottonwood Road, 1 mile off US 97, about 13 miles south of Bend; (541) 593-2421
tinyurl.com/lavarivercaveoregon

This mile-long cave formed when a lava flow cooled on its surface, but the lava below continued to flow. This created a hollow straw-shaped structure: a lava tube. Today, the lava is long-cooled, and you can descend down 55 uneven, rocky steps and tour the lava tube (in season). If you're planning a trip, bring warm clothes, sturdy shoes, and several light sources. There are multiple "rooms" to see here, and taken together, this is an impressive, eerie sight.

3 Oregon Caves National Monument and Preserve

19000 Caves Highway, Cave Junction 97523; (541) 592-2100
nps.gov/orca/index.htm

Elijah Davidson was the first person known to enter the wonderful caves here. Davidson was a hunter who first entered the caves in

1874. He did so while chasing after his dog, which in turn had chased a bear into the caverns. Not long thereafter, poet Joaquin Miller dubbed the caves "The Marble Halls of Oregon" and lobbied on their behalf. The site soon became a national monument in 1909. Today, the caves preserve an underground creek, as well as what remains of the cave stalactites, stalagmites, and columns that weren't damaged by early visitors. The site offers a variety of caving tours—from a Discovery Tour and a candlelight tour to one for Kids and Families. If you really want to see what caving is like, look up the Off-Trail Caving Tour, which is pretty intense. Aboveground, the national monument has hiking trails that wind through fir forests; one trail, appropriately known as the Big Tree Trail, winds past the widest Douglas-fir in all of Oregon. *Note:* The caves are not ADA accessible, and there are mobility requirements, so check online before booking a ticket.

4 Redmond Caves

Airport Way, Redmond 97756; (541) 416-6700
blm.gov/visit/redmond-caves-recreation-site

This is a unique and entirely accessible caving site. Located within the Redmond city limits, it's less than a mile from the Redmond Municipal Airport and numerous restaurants. These caves were produced by lava flows from the Newberry caldera, and they've been frequented by wildlife and people for thousands of years. Archaeological evidence indicates people have frequented these caves for at least 6,000 years. As with any cave, bring multiple light sources, and dress warmly. Also, keep in mind that these are natural caves, so watch out for rattlesnakes and other creatures.

5 Sea Lion Caves

91560 US 101 N., Florence 97439; (541) 547-3111
sealioncaves.com

This privately operated sea cave and its surroundings are a year-round home for Steller sea lions, birds, and other wildlife. This cave is not a zoo—you descend for an underground look at a large colony of sea lions; there are also informative displays on-site. The sea lions are most often in the cave in spring and winter, but when you visit it's not guaranteed that they'll be present, so call ahead to see if they're in the cave first. If they aren't, discount tickets are available, and the descent into the cave itself is exciting (it's big!). And though the sea lions are adorable, be forewarned that the smell might catch you off-guard.

Coquille River Lighthouse

WITH ITS ROCKY CLIFFS, powerful currents, hidden reefs, and treacherous tides, it's probably not surprising that Oregon's coast is the final resting place of many shipwrecks, most of which foundered before the advent of modern technology. Oregonians responded by building a number of lighthouses; today there are 11 in all still standing on the coasts. Here are a few of the more accessible and well-known.

LIGHTHOUSES

1 Cape Blanco State Park

91100 Cape Blanco Road, Port Orford 97465; (541) 332-6774
tinyurl.com/capeblancostatepark

Built in 1870, Cape Blanco was built because the cape's high winds, dangerous reefs, and often-foul weather provided a real threat to shipping. In fact, a shipwreck occurred here during the construction of the lighthouse—a vessel carrying supplies for the lighthouse sank and had to be replaced before the site was complete. As the westernmost place in Oregon, and the second-westernmost place in the continental U.S. (after Cape Alava, Washington), it was a difficult place to work and live. But it was important for shipping, and it still operates today as a working lighthouse. Today, Cape Blanco is perhaps best known for its pretty staggering scenery (the lighthouse towers over the sea), as well as a historic Victorian home built by a farmer that is now open for tours. After your tour, you can hike down to the beach, fish, or camp.

Note: Check the website for tour schedules (which are seasonal) and rates.

2 Cape Meares Lighthouse

Cape Meares State Scenic Viewpoint 2375 Cape Meares Loop, Tillamook 97141; (503) 842-3182

The view from Cape Meares is flat-out staggering. The lighthouse here was built in 1889, and unlike many other lighthouses, it's not especially tall. On the contrary, it's an oddity, as it's "only" 38 feet tall. Then again, perched on a cliff that is more than 200 feet above the water, it didn't need to be especially tall. Tours of the lighthouse are free, but check the website for seasonal information and weather info. The area is also great for viewing wildlife: whales can be spotted at various times in the year (migration seasons are December and January, March and April, and during summer). Seabirds, especially common murres and cormorants, are a common sight from spring into summer, and there are several short hiking trails and interpretive displays. One popular landmark is the Octopus Tree, a sprawling spruce that makes for a great photo op. While you're in the area, check out the other scenic spots on the Three Capes Scenic Loop; Cape Meares is just one of them.

3 Coquille River Lighthouse

Bullards Beach State Park Bullards Beach Road off US 101 (Oregon Coast Highway), Bandon 97411; (541) 347-2209
tinyurl.com/bullardsbeach

The Coquille River, named after the Native American tribe that has resided in the area for thousands of years, was once a prominent shipping hazard. The currents and winds near the river's mouth were often treacherous, and the shifting sand bar it created made it easy for ships to run aground. Recognizing the threat, the Coast Guard built a lighthouse and a jetty on-site, but even today, with a modern jetty in place, entering the harbor can be tricky. The lighthouse, first operational in 1896, is something of an oddity in that its base is octagonal. It operated until 1939 and was abandoned for more than two decades; it was eventually restored and is now part of Bullards Beach State Park. Today, visitors can tour the lighthouse's signal room (but not the tower) from mid-May through September. The park also has miles of beach to explore, and the area is famous as a storm-watching destination.

4 Tillamook Rock Lighthouse

Ecola State Park About 2 miles north of Cannon Beach and about 1 mile north off US 101 (Oregon Coast Highway); (503) 812-0650; tinyurl.com/ecolastateparkor

Visible in the distance from a viewpoint at Ecola State Park, Tillamook Rock Lighthouse is situated a mile from shore. It had an inauspicious start when a would-be designer of the lighthouse, John Trewavas, was brought out to the rock; he slipped when trying to step onto the rock, and then drowned. Nonetheless, the project moved forward, and eventually a lighthouse was built, 90 feet above the sea. Despite this great height, it was not immune from the wrath of the ocean. On the contrary, winter storms wreaked havoc on the lighthouse, and its keepers, with boulders being flung into the lighthouse and water cascading into the rooms. Not surprisingly, the lighthouse keepers were under immense stress (physically and mentally), and the lighthouse soon earned the nickname "Terrible Tilly," with many keepers quitting or being removed due to the mental strain. Seawater from one massive storm in the 1930s even put out the lighthouse's beacon, though it was restored soon thereafter. The lighthouse operated until 1957 and then cycled through a number of owners. The most recent owners turned the lighthouse into a columbarium—a repository for cremated remains— but that venture was relatively short-lived. Today, the lighthouse is in rough shape, and, for obvious reasons, tours aren't available.

5 Umpqua Lighthouse

Umpqua Lighthouse State Park 1020 Lighthouse Road, Winchester Bay 97467;
(541) 271-4118
tinyurl.com/umpqualighthouse

The first lighthouse built here began operating in 1857 as part of an effort to protect the ships of the area's nascent lumber industry. When construction began, this lighthouse was very unpopular with the area's Indigenous inhabitants, who had lived in the area for thousands of years. They responded by using nonviolent measures—stealing tools—to slow down the construction process. Violent storms also delayed construction, but the lighthouse was eventually lit in 1857. That lighthouse wouldn't last long, however, as storms and river floods wrecked the foundation, alarming the lighthouse keepers and eventually toppling the entire structure. In 1894, a new lighthouse—this one built on safer ground—began operating, and it's still lit today; its original Fresnel lens is even still in use. The lighthouse is operated by the county parks department, and it also features a museum, which is housed in a historic Coast Guard building. Tours are available from May through October and by appointment in the winter. As you might expect, the weather here can get a bit interesting, so check the forecast and make sure to dress warmly in winter.

6 Yaquina Head & Yaquina Bay Lighthouses

Yaquina Head Lighthouse Yaquina Head Outstanding Natural Area, 750 NW
Lighthouse Drive, Newport 97365; (541) 574-3100
blm.gov/learn/interpretive-centers/yaquina

Yaquina Bay Lighthouse Yaquina Bay State Recreation Site, 846 SW Government
St., Newport 97365; (541) 265-5679
tinyurl.com/yaquinabay

Newport is home to not one but two lighthouses, including Oregon's tallest, Yaquina Head Lighthouse, which has a tower that reaches 93 feet. Yaquina Head Lighthouse was first lit in 1873, and it has been an Oregon destination for decades. Part of its allure is its sheer grandeur, but it also is cloaked in legend, as it is reputedly haunted (though by whom seems to vary with each telling). One eerie feature of Yaquina Head is absolutely true: ships that get too close to the cliff on which it's perched will see any traditional compasses go haywire.

There's a relatively simple explanation for this: the rocks beneath it are made of magnetized iron, a material that interferes with magnetic compasses. Tours of Yaquina Head are offered throughout the year when possible, but call ahead for dates, times, and what to expect. Once you're done, check out the tide pools at the base of Yaquina Head; there you can see starfish, urchins, and other sea life. (Check the website for information on schedules and safety tips.)

The Yaquina Bay Lighthouse has a strange history. It first started operating in 1871, but it was shuttered, and then abandoned, just three years later. The Yaquina Head Lighthouse, first lit in 1873, was in a better location, making the initial lighthouse obsolete. The lighthouse was practically falling apart within a few years. It was repaired shortly thereafter, but it wasn't used for more than a decade, when the U.S. Army Corps and, later, the U.S. Life-Saving Service (and its successor, the Coast Guard) began using the structure (but never actually as a lighthouse). Eventually, the lighthouse was donated to the State of Oregon in the 1930s, and for the next few decades it was always on the cusp of being demolished. Happily, lighthouse fans came together to vouch on its behalf, and it was eventually not only saved, but restored and relit, becoming a private aid to navigation. It's now part of Yaquina Bay State Recreation Site, which offers tours (check the website for seasonal schedules) and hiking and is a great spot for whale-watching.

The top of the historic Umpqua Lighthouse

A Rainbow Lorakeet at the Portland Zoo

GATHER THE FAMILY to explore everything the Beaver State has to offer, from historic amusement parks and water parks to wild-animal sanctuaries, enchanted forests, and aquariums and zoos.

FAMILY DAY

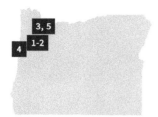

1 Enchanted Forest

8462 Enchanted Way SE, Turner 97392; (503) 371-4242
enchantedforest.com

Nursery rhymes come to life at this delightful theme park. The brain-child of Robert Tofte, Enchanted Forest is a life-size introduction to famous children's stories, the Wild West, and more. It all started with Storybook Lane, which Tofte built by hand. There, you'll find Humpty Dumpty; you can also walk through a castle and climb through the rabbit hole from *Alice in Wonderland*. There's also a Wild West Town, rides, animatronic animals, whimsical statues, and more. An area tradition for families of little ones for generations, Enchanted Forest has an endearingly quirky charm.

2 The Gilbert House Children's Museum

116 Marion St. NE, Salem 97301; (503) 371-3631
acgilbert.org

This children's museum is dedicated to "learning through creative play," and appropriately enough, it's named after A. C. Gilbert, a native of Salem and the inventor of the Erector Set, who was well-known for his popular line of chemistry sets (some of which contained actual radioactive materials), magic kits, and more. The Gilbert House mirrors the hands-on approach found in Gilbert's toys and includes immersive exhibits where kids can play and learn about farming and food production, medicine, the arts, and engineering. There's a television studio with a real green screen, a veterinarian's office, and a massive outdoor play space, among many other fun attractions. The Gilbert House Children's Museum is recommended for kids ages 2–10, though older siblings and parents often have as much fun as the little ones.

3 Oaks Amusement Park

7805 SE Oaks Park Way, Portland 97202; (503) 233-5777
oakspark.com

For over a century, Oaks Amusement Park has offered Oregonians a place to escape. Originally a "trolley park" that opened in 1905 to entertain streetcar riders, it originally featured rides, fireworks, and a bathing area. Plus, one of its main features was a then-newfangled invention: electric lighting!

The attractions have changed since then, but the basic premise at Oaks Park is still the same: family fun. With indoor roller-skating offered year-round, along with rides and games in the warmer months, there's a lot to do on-site. Riders can take in a classic 1912 carousel, blast off on a roller-coaster, or try their luck at carnival-style games. There's also a seasonal 18-hole miniature golf course. If you're visiting in the winter, roller-skating is offered indoors year-round, with rental skates available on-site.

4 Oregon Coast Aquarium

2820 SE Ferry Slip Road, Newport 97365; (541) 867-3474
aquarium.org

With more than a dozen main exhibits, including an underwater tunnel where you can see sharks, rays, and other critters swimming by, this aquarium is a perfect introduction to the wide variety of animals and plants found on the Oregon Coast. The museum is home to crabs, octopuses, jellyfish, sea stars, and clownfish, as well as sea otters, seals, sea lions, and seabirds. Before you visit, check the website for the feeding schedule for the otters, sea lions, and birds, and for the aquarium's pelican presentations. Don't miss the aquarium's touch tanks, and read up on the animal encounters it offers for an extra fee; at those, you can snag a photo op with a giant Pacific octopus or touch sea jellies.

And if you're scuba-certified, you can actually suit up and dive in the aquarium. (*Note:* A dive for one person costs about $250.) Once you're done touring the exhibits, take a stroll on the on-site nature trail, where there are several locations to get a glimpse of the Yaquina Bay estuary.

Fish at the Oregon Coast Aquarium

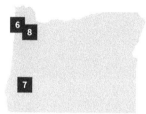

5 Oregon Zoo

4001 SW Canyon Road, Portland 97221; (503) 226-1561
oregonzoo.org

Covering 64 acres, this Pacific Northwest standard has recently
undergone a massive upgrade, and many of its main exhibits have
been refreshed or even revamped entirely. With a mix of animals
native to the Pacific Northwest and those found far afield, it's home
to everything from polar bears and elephants to tigers, California
condors and even Australian walking sticks. For a behind-the-scenes
look at the some of the zoo's animals, check out its Wild Connections
program; for an extra fee, you can meet various zoo denizens, from
tarantulas and leaf insects to owls, giraffes, and lemurs. (The rules,
activities, and prices vary by experience, but all include an up-close
look at an animal and the chance to take photos. In some cases,
you can feed or even touch the animals.) The zoo also offers a wide
variety of programs, classes, and camps for kids and school groups.

6 Tillamook Creamery

4165 US 101 N., Tillamook 97141; (503) 815-1300
tillamook.com/creamery.html

Tillamook dairy products are a Pacific Northwest institution. In
operation since 1909, the company is a cooperative that's farmer
owned, and its products—but especially its cheese—are available
in many places throughout the country. The free self-guided tour
introduces visitors to what life is like on a dairy farm, lets them get
a look at the factory in action from the viewing gallery, and, best of
all, gives them the chance to sample fresh cheese. After the tour,
there's a café with tasty food options that incorporate Tillamook
products, including several types of mac and cheese, sandwiches,
and *an entire menu devoted to ice cream.* After you eat, there's a gift
shop with all sorts of Tillamook swag.

7 Wildlife Safari

1790 Safari Road, Winston 97496; (541) 679-6761
wildlifesafari.net

Wildlife Safari is essentially a zoo, but in reverse. The animals here originate from three continents, and on this driving tour, humans are the ones sequestered to a tiny enclosure: a car! The animals here are largely free to wander where they like, so don't be surprised if you see a rhino blocking the road, a curious emu sidling up to your passenger-side window, or the like. With animals from Asia, Africa, and the Americas, you'll see everything from giraffes and lions to brown bears, African elephants, and yaks. The site also has a free petting zoo with farmyard animals, as well as animal encounters where you can see elephants, giraffes, bears, or the organization's famous cheetahs, up close. Best of all, the folks at Wildlife Safari also have some serious conservation chops; in fact, Wildlife Safari is the site of the most successful cheetah-breeding program in the US.

8 Wings & Waves Waterpark

460 NE Captain Michael King Smith Way, McMinnville 97128; (503) 687-3390
wingsandwaveswaterpark.com

Evergreen Aviation is a now-defunct cargo airline with long Oregon ties. Based out of McMinnville, the airline preserves its legacy in one of the oddest—and coolest—water parks around. A real Evergreen Boeing 747 jet is perched on the roof of the building, and the belly of the plane is actually the starting point for a number of waterslides. The park has five main waterslides in all, and they have names like Sonic Boom, Tail Spin, and Mach 1. There are also slides better suited for younger folks, a vortex pool, a leisure pool, and a hot tub. There's also on-site food, and next door (additional ticket required) is the Evergreen Aviation Museum (see page 24), home to the famous *Spruce Goose* and a host of other aircraft.

The famous Haystack Rock on Cannon Beach

WITH MORE THAN 360 MILES of coastline on the Pacific Ocean, Oregon has practically countless beaches and endless opportunities for beachcombing, rockhounding, and relaxing. If you can brave the usually cold water, surfing's even an option. Many restaurants feature fresh seafood, saltwater taffy, and small-town atmospheres.

Safety alert: Oregon coasts are notorious for so-called sneaker waves—large waves that can strike without warning. *Never turn your back on the ocean.* Also, before you head out, check the tide tables for the beach you'll be visiting.

BEACHES &
BEACH TOWNS

1 Astoria

Astoria Warrenton Chamber of Commerce 111 W. Marine Drive, Astoria 97103;
(503) 325-6311
astoriaoregon.com, travelastoria.com

Victorian homes line the hills of this small city, which offers both a
rich history and modern convenience. For example, a craft brewery
is located just down the street from the historic Liberty Theater,
built in the 1920s as a vaudeville venue. Known as "the little San
Francisco" because of the many fortunes once made there and its
opulent architecture, today Astoria is known for good food; a fascinating, quirky side; and, of course, ready beach access. Sunset Beach
Recreation Area is just minutes away, and another nearby beach, in
Warrenton, boasts a famous shipwreck, the *Peter Iredale,* which you
can walk up to at low tide (see page 66 for more information). And if
you visit Astoria and find that certain buildings or houses look familiar to you, they just might be: portions of *Free Willy, The Goonies,
Kindergarten Cop,* and *Short Circuit* were all filmed here.

2 Cannon Beach

Cannon Beach Visitor Information Center & Chamber of Commerce 207 N.
Spruce St., Cannon Beach 97110, (503) 436-2623
cannonbeach.org

Cannon Beach is 4 miles long and home to one of the coast's most
famous formations: Haystack Rock, a towering sea stack that's a
common sight on postcards and in magazines, and for good reason.
It's stunning, and it's also surrounded by tide pools with sea stars
and other ocean life that are fascinating to explore when the tides
are right (usually in spring and summer). (These are also protected
areas, so please tread gently and only on bare sand or rock.) In
addition to the tide pools and their inhabitants, the beach is also a
birding hot spot, and it's famous for its colorful puffins (which nest
on top of Haystack Rock) and common murres. Cannon Beach is also
a great place to visit in June, as it holds the longest-running sandcas-
tle contest in the Pacific Northwest. Once you're done on the beach,
the town is completely walkable and has brewpubs, restaurants, art
galleries, and cute shops to keep you busy.

3 Depoe Bay

Depoe Bay Visitor Center & Chamber of Commerce 223 SW US 101, Depoe Bay
97341; (541) 765-2889, (877) 485-8348
discoverdepoebay.org, visittheoregoncoast.com/cities/depoe-bay

Depoe Bay couldn't get any closer to the ocean: the town is bordered
by the rocky shore and a rough seawall. It's an easy place to find a
great ocean view, but the town proper doesn't have sandy beaches.
Instead, it's rocky and wild. When the weather gets bumpy, water
in the "spouting horn" here shoots into the air for dozens of feet,
sometimes drenching observers and even cars on US 101, which cuts
through town. (But don't get too close for a photo, as the ledges can
be dangerous and storms have swept people away here.) Depoe Bay
is also well-known as a whale-watching hot spot. Depoe Bay is also
famous for its tiny 6-acre harbor, with signs proclaiming it "The World's
Smallest Harbor."

4 Gold Beach

Gold Beach Visitor Center 94080 Shirley Lane, Gold Beach 97444; (541) 247-7526;
visitgoldbeach.com

A two-stoplight town with access to the Rogue River, old-growth
forests, and sandy shores, Gold Beach is a popular destination for
beachcombing for agates, jasper, and jade, and its shores also have
tide pools, copious driftwood, and plenty of solitude. The beach gets
its name because small amounts of gold were discovered here in
the 1850s. That mini–gold rush petered out, but commercial salmon
fishing and, later, sport fishing, became a major draw. Fishing, beachcombing, windsurfing, and kayaking are all popular today. If you visit,
you may find yourself alone on a beach, mesmerized by the waves and
the wind. Better yet, there are plenty of beaches to try out and ready
access points throughout town.

5 Moolack Beach

About 4.5 miles north of Newport; GPS: 44.69983, -124.06539

Most accessible at low tide, this undeveloped beach is a rockhound's
dream, as it's well-known for sea glass, agates, and even fossils of
snails and shells. The best time to collect such finds is in winter, as the
beach is often covered in more sand in summer. Occasionally whale
bones and other vertebrate fossils are seen on the beach, though collecting those is illegal. A stroll down Moolack Beach leads to several
other notable sights, including Yaquina Head Lighthouse, 2 miles to
the south (see page 48), and Devils Punchbowl State Natural Area,
4 miles to the north, where a pair of collapsed sea caves has created a

bowl-like structure where waves swirl and crash when the tides are right. At low tide, you can venture down into the punchbowl itself.

6 Neskowin Beach

Neskowin Beach State Recreation Site US 101 (Oregon Coast Highway), Neskowin 97149; GPS: 45.10024, -123.98124; (541) 994-7341
tinyurl.com/neskowinbeach, neskowinoregon.com, tillamookcoast.com
/where-to-go/neskowin

Neskowin Beach is both scenic and eerie. Its long stretch of gorgeous beach is home to the remnants of an ill-fated "ghost forest" that was buried and preserved here, probably by a tsunami or an earthquake, about 2,000 years ago. The forest was uncovered in the late 1990s after a series of severe storms. Today, it can be seen only during low or negative tides. The beach is also home to tide pools, sea stacks, and several hiking options at Neskowin Beach State Recreation Site. Adjacent to the beach, the unincorporated town of Neskowin (population 170) offers lodging, golf, and gorgeous views.

7 Port Orford

City of Port Orford Visitor Center 520 Jefferson St., Port Orford 97465; (541) 332-4106
portorford.org/visitor-center

As Europeans settled in Oregon in the middle of the 19th century, Native Americans in the area took exception to their territory being claimed, especially since the law that led to Oregon settlement—the Oregon Donation Land Act—hadn't been agreed to or signed by any of these Indigenous peoples. This often led to conflict, and one of the landmarks in Port Orford is the site of one such battle. Its Battle Rock Park is the location of a skirmish between the Qua-To-Mah tribe and the initial settlers who took up a defensive position on Battle Rock, a sea stack. The settlers eventually won a bloody battle, and Port Orford was founded as a town in 1852.

Like many towns on the Oregon coast, Port Orford has long ties to the fishing and timber industries, and fishing remains important in town today. Tourism is also a major draw, and there's a lot to see—from the unique port, which doesn't actually have any boats sitting in the water (instead, they're lifted out using a large crane) to hiking options, whale-watching, and, just west of town, Port Orford Heads State Park, home to the Port Orford Lifeboat Station, now a museum that's open seasonally. In town, you can also visit the historic Hughes House, a restored Victorian home built in 1898. As you might expect, there are also plenty of places where you access the nearby coast.

8 Rockaway Beach

Rockaway Beach Visitors Center   103 S. First St., Rockaway Beach 97136, (503) 355-8108
rockawaybeach.net

Rockaway Beach is essentially one long beach town. With 7 miles of sandy beach in all, and many access points (including several with parking), getting here is easy, and there's a lot to do. You can't miss the impressive sea stacks—known as the Twin Rocks—if you look at the right angle, you'll notice one of the rocks has an arch. The beach is also popular for kite flying, whale-watching (during migration season), and kayaking on calm days. In town, there are restaurants, antiques stores, gift shops, and more.

9 Short Sand Beach

Oswald West State Park   US 101 (Oregon Coast Highway), Arch Cape 97102; GPS: 45.77527, -123.94555; (503) 368-3575
tinyurl.com/oswaldwestsp

About 2 miles north of the town of Manzanita, this small, sandy beach (dubbed "Shorty's" by locals) is surrounded by Smuggler's Cove. To get to the beach, start from Oswald West State Park's main lot, then walk through a picturesque forest to reach the beach. This is a popular beach for surfing and boogie boarding, and two hiking trails are accessible from the beach, with several more (including one adventurous 6.5-mile hike) in the vicinity. See the park's website for a handy brochure with a map.

Pittock Mansion

NATIVE AMERICANS HAVE LIVED in what is now known as Oregon for thousands of years. Lewis and Clark first saw the beauty of Oregon in 1805. By the 1840s, settlers traveling on the Oregon Trail streamed into the state, changing it forever. Much of the state's history is well preserved, so whether you're looking to walk part of the original Oregon Trail, see a shipwreck, or visit a ghost town, it's all here.

HISTORIC OREGON

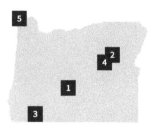

1 Fort Rock State Natural Area

County Rd 5-11A, Fort Rock 97735; GPS: 43.37076,-121.06596; (800) 551-6949
tinyurl.com/fortrockstatenaturalarea

True to its name, Fort Rock almost looks human-made. The stadium-like geological feature is known as a tuff ring. It formed around 100,000 years ago when magma made contact with water, resulting in dramatic explosions, rapidly cooling rock, and the creation of 200-foot-tall cliffs. A guided tour is the only way to explore the site and learn about the long geological and human history of the area: the surrounding land was once covered by a shallow sea, and Fort Rock was an island. That island was visited by ancient Indigenous peoples; a pair of sandals found nearby date back perhaps 13,000 years. While you're there, visit the nearby Homestead Village Museum. It's home to a number of well-preserved historic buildings from the surrounding area, including a one-room schoolhouse.

2 Greenhorn

Greenhorn Road (Road 503B), about 28 miles west of Sumpter; GPS: 44.70931, -118.49651; (541) 894-2472
historicsumpter.com/greenhorn-oregon-ghost-town

Situated high up in the Blue Mountains (6,306 feet above sea level), Greenhorn has a similar story to that of many other ghost towns: it was a mining boomtown that had a promising start, followed by a population crash that never rebounded. Today, its population is zero, but somewhat amazingly, it still has a mayor and a city council. Visitors often come in the summer to see its vintage wooden buildings. One building, however, has been missing since 1963: the tiny town jail. In perhaps the oddest prank on record, someone moved the entire jail and deposited it nearby Canyon City, where it remains to this day.

Note: Friends of the Sumpter Valley Gold Dredge, a historic-preservation organization, provides turn-by-turn driving directions for getting here from the town of Sumpter at its website above, along with a custom Google map of the route. If you're coming from points north, they also recommend taking along the U.S.

Forest Service's *North Fork John Day Ranger District* map, available at the USGS Store (store.usgs.gov/maps) and Avenza Maps (avenzamaps.com).

3 Jacksonville

Jacksonville Chamber of Commerce & Visitor Information Center 185 N. Oregon St., Jacksonville 97530; (541) 899-8118
jacksonvilleoregon.org

Jacksonville started out as a mining boomtown, and for a time it was an economic powerhouse in southern Oregon. Things changed when the railroad bypassed the town, leading to a long-running economic decline. That decision, however, had a major silver lining: the town's original architecture remained unaltered, and today the entire town is protected as a National Historic Landmark. It's literally like going back in time. Despite its size, the town is brimming with things to do, from Segway and trolley tours to myriad wine-tasting rooms and more.

4 Kam Wah Chung State Heritage Center

125 NW Canton St., John Day 97845; (541) 575-2800
friendsofkamwahchung.com

In the late 1880s, two Chinese immigrants, Lung On and Ing "Doc" Hay, turned what was once a trading post in John Day into a pharmacy for Chinese traditional medicine, a doctor's office, and a meeting place. The building is preserved as a National Historic Landmark to memorialize the massive impact that Chinese immigrants have had on the history of Oregon and the Pacific Northwest. It now features a museum, where you can see the largest collection of Chinese herbal medicines and formulas in the world, as well as an interpretive center, gift shop, and tours.

5 Lewis & Clark National Historical Park

Fort Clatsop Visitor Center 92343 Fort Clatsop Road, Astoria 97103; (503) 861-2471
nps.gov/lewi

In 1804, President Thomas Jefferson tasked Meriwether Lewis and William Clark with exploring the lands he'd recently acquired from the French in the Louisiana Purchase. Lewis and Clark trekked by river from St. Louis to the Pacific, along with 31 others, including Sacagawea, a Shoshone woman who helped guide the expedition, and York, an African American enslaved by William Clark. The group made their winter camp at what they dubbed Fort Clatsop, a wooden fort they named after a local Indigenous tribe. In all, the group spent three months on-site, and today you can enjoy a replica of the original fort, living-history demonstrations, and plenty of hiking and sightseeing opportunities.

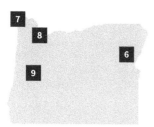

6 National Historic Oregon Trail Interpretive Center

22267 OR 86, Baker City 97814, (541) 523-1843
nps.gov/oreg/planyourvisit/national-oregon-trail-center.htm

If you're of a certain age, there's a chance that you played the vintage video game *Oregon Trail*. Famously difficult, it was an introduction for millions to the real-world trials and tribulations that played out 150 years before on the real Oregon Trail, which led about 2,000 miles from Missouri to the fertile Willamette River Valley. This interpretive center is located in what was once the home stretch of the Oregon Trail, about 300 miles from the valley. Here, you can see the remnants of the Oregon Trail itself—including several miles of wagon ruts. The site's interpretive center also has living-history demonstrations, dioramas, and an interpretive trail system.

7 *Peter Iredale* Shipwreck

Port Stevens State Park 100 *Peter Iredale* Road, Hammond 97121;
(503) 861-3170
tinyurl.com/fortstevensstatepark

The *Peter Iredale* was a steel cargo vessel that was set to deliver a load of grain from the United Kingdom to Portland. (It was named after the man who owned the ship, which was part of his Liverpool, England–based fleet.) As it entered the mouth of the Columbia River on October 25, 1906, a heavy fog rolled in. The ship's captain opted to wait for a pilot, and as they did the wind began gusting and the current pushed the ship aground. Thanks to some daring work by the local lifesaving station, the crew was all rescued, but the ship was a total wreck. Today, at low tide, the ship is a tourist attraction, and while it's now just a rusted hulk, it's a reminder of the state's nautical history and the sheer power of the ocean. The wreck is located in what is now Fort Stevens State Park.

8 Pittock Mansion

3229 NW Pittock Drive, Portland 97210, (503) 823-3623
pittockmansion.org

This French Renaissance–style mansion was built in 1914 by newspaper magnate and businessman Henry Pittock, who moved west in the 1850s via the Oregon Trail and worked as a typesetter for *The Oregonian*. He soon became owner of the paper, which thrived (and still exists today), and he also diversified his business interests, investing in everything from livestock to mining. In 1914, the 16,000-square-foot mansion was built, complete with 23 rooms, and the latest technology at the time, such as electric lighting, central heat, and an elevator. Pittock died only a few years after his mansion was completed; it stayed in the family for decades and was eventually heavily damaged in a 1962 windstorm. The house came close to being demolished, but the community and donors stepped in and restored it, and it's now owned by the city.

9 University Hall

University of Oregon 1585 E. 13th Ave., Eugene 97403; (541) 346-1000
library.uoregon.edu/architecture/oregon/deady

The sloping sides of an iconic mansard roof crown University Hall, home of the University of Oregon's math department. Designed by William W. Piper and built from 1873 to 1878, this Italianate–Second Empire structure was the University of Oregon's first—and for nearly a decade—only building on campus. When it opened, "The Building," as it was originally known, didn't just educate college-age students: it was the only educational facility of any kind in Eugene, and it actually served more students in elementary school and high school than those in college. As the campus grew, "The Building" became known as the "Old Building," but in 1893 it was informally named Deady Hall after the death that year of Matthew Deady, a prominent lawyer and state legislator who had served as president of the university's board of regents and helped establish its law school. Deady Hall became the building's official name in 1926.

Deady served as a Supreme Court justice of the Oregon Territory and later as a U.S. district judge; less impressively, however, he codified racism into state law as the president of Oregon's first constitutional convention in 1857. Voters rejected his proposal to make slavery legal in Oregon, but they did approve a provision making it illegal for Black people to live in the state. Although the law was never actually enforced and was nullified by the 14th Amendment to the U.S. Constitution in 1868, it wasn't officially stricken from the Oregon Constitution

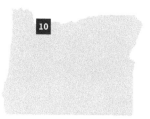

until 1926. In 2020, after several years of mounting student protests, the university's board of trustees voted unanimously to temporarily change the name of Deady Hall to University Hall (the new name has not yet been chosen at the time of this writing).

10 Vista House at the Gorge

40700 E. Historic Columbia River Highway, Corbett 97060; (503) 344-1368
vistahouse.com

Situated along the mighty Columbia River, Vista House is a magnificent structure perched atop Crown Point. Built in 1917, this stunning eight-sided building offers the best of both worlds: fine architecture and natural scenery and views to match. Built after the construction of US Highway 30 (now the Historic Columbia River Highway), Vista House was intended as a scenic viewpoint, a rest stop, and a means of commemorating the history of Oregon's pioneers. Now preserved as a National Natural Landmark, its stunning architecture and 360-degree views make it a must-see.

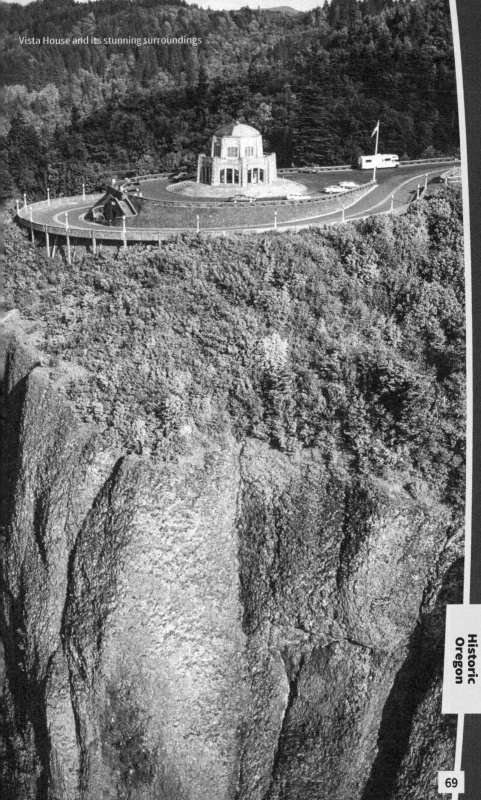

Vista House and its stunning surroundings

The otherworldly Dee Wright Observatory and its moonscape-like surroundings

MEMORABLY SKEWERED IN THE SITCOM *Portlandia,*
aggressive quirkiness isn't just a thing in Portland—it's a way of
life. The city certainly lives up to its unofficial motto of "Keep It
Weird," but there are plenty more strange spots scattered across
the state. Here's a rundown of just some of the odd things Oregon
has to offer.

KEEP IT WEIRD

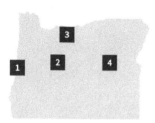

1 Darlingtonia State Natural Site

5400 Mercer Lake Road, Florence 97439; (541) 997-3851
tinyurl.com/darlingtoniastatenaturalsite

State parks usually exist to preserve and protect a wide variety of plants and animals. Not at Darlingtonia State Natural Site. It primarily exists to protect one plant species: *Darlington californica,* also known as the cobra lily. The only type of pitcher plant found in Oregon, the plant deserves its somewhat intimidating name, as it is carnivorous. Its odd, vase-like leaves attract insects, which then fall into the pitcher-like leaves, where they die and are digested by bacteria that live inside the plant. The park features a boardwalk across the fen where the plants are found, as well as a small picnic area. For obvious reasons, collecting specimens is strictly forbidden, but photos are welcome.

Darlington californica, Darlingtonia State Natural Site

2 Dee Wright Observatory

McKenzie Highway (OR 242), 15 miles west of Sisters, Blue River 97413;
GPS: 44.2318, -121.8680; (800) 832-1355
tinyurl.com/deewrightobservatory

Perched atop the Cascades at 5,187 feet in elevation and located between a pair of wilderness areas (and just east of a stretch of the Pacific Crest Trail), Dee Wright Observatory is a wonderful stop to take in the scenery of the gorgeous surroundings and marvel at the otherworldly lava flows that flowed here some 3,000 years ago. The observatory itself—a stone structure worthy of *Lord of the Rings*—was built by the Civilian Conservation Corps in 1935; interpretive signage describes the area's geological and volcanic history and identifies the many peaks visible on-site. If you visit and think it looks like a different planet, you're not alone: NASA astronauts once trained here in preparation for the lunar landings.

Note: McKenzie Highway (OR 242) closes in winter (November–July) due to snowfall, so make sure the road is open before you head out.

3 Friend Ghost Town

Friend, Heberlein, and Friend Store Roads, about 15 miles southeast of Dufur; GPS: 45.3467, -121.2672
atlasobscura.com/places/friend-ghost-town

Once situated at the end of the Great Southern Railroad line, the tiny town of Friend, Oregon, was effectively abandoned after the railway folded due to competition with cars and busses. While the people of Friend left soon thereafter, some of the Great Depression–era buildings still remain. A one-room schoolhouse still stands, as do a general store and attached post office, scattered farm buildings, and a cemetery where George J. Friend, the town's namesake, is buried.

4 The Humongous Fungus

Malheur National Forest 8.5 miles south of US 26, Prairie City 97869 (approximately bounded by Forest Service Road 026 to the west and Forest Service Road 2635 to the east); GPS: 44.47617, -118.48477; (541) 820-3800
tinyurl.com/thehumongousfungus

If someone asked you to identify the largest living thing on Earth, you might say the blue whale, or maybe the African elephant. But you'd be wrong. It's actually a fungus, known scientifically as *Armillaria ostoyae* and commonly as the honey mushroom. And no, it doesn't look like what you might be visualizing right about now (say, a prop mushroom from *Honey, I Shrunk the Kids*). There are five distinct colonies of this fungus in Malheur National Forest; the largest of these—more than 12,000 feet wide and covering nearly 2,400 acres—is affectionately known as "the humongous fungus."

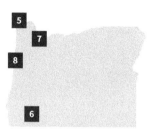

Armillaria ostoyae is a pathogen of trees, and it has spent the past several thousand years slowly consuming the forest here. Most of the time, you likely won't see actual mushrooms with caps and stems; instead, the fungus is most visible as a slimy, thread-like white substance—earning it the alternate common name of shoe-string fungus—in the soil or in the root systems of toppled trees. If you were to peel the bark off an affected tree, you'd find it there, too, but don't do that (see below). Perhaps even more impressive than the humongous fungus's size is its age: the U.S. Forest Service estimates that it may be up to 8,650 years old.

Safety note: Because this is a plant–pathogenic fungal species, the trees it feeds on are often dead or dying, meaning that limbs or trees can fall without warning, so keep a safe distance. Also, be aware that the fungus is located in a remote part of the forest where cell service is iffy—we've listed the GPS coordinates provided by the USFS, but instead of relying solely on your phone, we strongly advise down-loading and printing out the brochure from the website above, which includes a map of the area with roads clearly labeled.

5 Museum of Whimsy

1215 Duane St., Astoria; (425) 417-6512
museumofwhimsy.com

This elegant Neoclassical-style building was once a bank, but today it holds something much more fitting for its elegant architecture: an assemblage of fascinating finds and curiosities collected over the years by Trish Bright, whose sense of wonder and style permeates the place. The exhibits change over time, so check back often to see what's new.

6 The Oregon Vortex and the House of Mystery

4303 Sardine Creek Left Fork Road, Gold Hill 97525; (541) 855-1543
oregonvortex.com

An old-time roadside attraction since the 1930s, the Oregon Vortex is relatively well-known in Oregon and beyond, having been featured on *History's Mysteries* and *Unsolved Mysteries* and even mentioned by Fox Mulder in an episode of *The X-Files*. The site was once a mining assay office, but today it's most famous for its (mostly self-made) mysterious backstory, and especially the optical illusions found on-site, which can make a figure appear to be taller or shorter depending on where they stand. The sensation is uncanny, making it a fun spot to snap photos (video recording is prohibited, though).

Note: At the time of this writing, no walk-in visits are allowed—you must reserve a tour (10 people maximum); check the website for details and updates.

7 Powell's City of Books

1005 W. Burnside St., Portland 97209; (503) 228-4651
powells.com/locations/powells-city-of-books

Powell's is a Portland institution. Once the site of a car dealership, Powell's main location (one of three) is home to a seemingly endless number of books, from paperback potboilers and romances to poetry, nonfiction, and rare treasures. To help you find your way around, the flagship store is organized by color-coded rooms. In addition to all those books, the stores are home to a wide variety of readings; signings; and appearances by authors, writers, and more. Originally run by a father–son team, the bookstore is now owned by Emily Powell and remains in the Powell family today.

8 Ripley's Believe It Or Not! and Louis Tussaud's Waxworks

250 SW Bay Blvd., Newport 97365; (541) 265-2206
marinersquare.com

Two adventures await you here. Ripley's Believe It or Not! is famous for the bizarre and the unbelievable. Robert Ripley wrote his first comic strip in 1918, and in it he introduced readers to the surreal, the bizarre, and the seemingly unbelievable—such as the fact that Charles Lindbergh wasn't the first person to cross the ocean by air. (He wasn't, but he was the first to do it solo.) Ripley soon became beloved and traveled the world, accumulating curiosities from the world over. This museum continues his legacy: you'll see a magic harp seemingly plucking its own strings, bizarre animals, and more. Tussaud's Waxworks, located next door, is another odd-but-fun stop. There, meticulously sculpted wax figures of Marilyn Monroe and other celebrities mingle with those of superheroes and television stars.

9 Voodoo Doughnut

22 SW Third Ave., Portland 97204; (503) 241-4704
voodoodoughnut.com

Voodoo Doughnut founders Kenneth "Cat Daddy" Pogson and Richard "Tres" Shannon founded this inventive, creative shop that meshes perfectly with Portland's status as the epicenter of all things hipster. From the start, Voodoo has offered both a number of tried-and-true doughnuts as well as a medley of adventurous, artistic, and just plain off-the-wall varieties, including a chocolate doughnut covered in Butterfinger candy; one made with Tang, vanilla, and marshmallows; and, this being Portland, one shaped like a large blunt and another that might make your grandma blush. Since its inception, Voodoo has expanded; there are now four locations in Oregon and several scattered across Colorado and Texas, along with outposts at Universal Studios Hollywood and Universal Orlando Resort in Florida.

10 World Naked Bike Ride

Portland
pdxwnbr.org

Held annually in June, the Naked Bike Ride is a worldwide event that has seemingly become more popular in Portland with each passing year. The first iteration in Portland was held in 2004 with just 125 riders, but over the past few years, it has seen tens of thousands of participants. While the Naked Bike Ride is often associated with Portland, it is held in many other cities as well. The rides were first held as an anti-war protest and later morphed into an anti-oil protest. Today, the rides still have something of a protest vibe, though the organizers emphasize other aspects of the ride, such as community building, self-sufficiency, and body awareness. To participate, you don't have to bike nude, or even shirtless; it's all about baring what you dare and finding your comfort level.

Options at Voodoo Doughnut range from the familiar to the eccentric, such as the candy- and breakfast cereal-topped doughnuts shown here

The Baldwin Hotel Museum

INDUCTED INTO THE UNION IN 1859, Oregon is one of the younger states, but it's chock-full of culture, history, and art, and its museums are a testament to that cultural and artistic heritage.

MUSEUMS

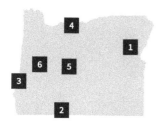

1 Baker Heritage Museum

2480 Grove St., Baker City 97814; (541) 523-9308
bakerheritagemuseum.com

In 1969, Clint Eastwood starred in *Paint Your Wagon,* a musical Western shot near Baker City. The movie didn't do well at the box office, but the film (and the seemingly exasperating way in which it was made) inspired Eastwood to start directing, and the museum recently celebrated its ties to the film with an exhibit to mark the 50th anniversary. There's more to the museum than movies, however. It documents the major industries that made Baker County, from mining and timber to ranching. Housed in a gorgeous 1920s-era building that was once the town natatorium (a public pool), it now houses a wide variety of artifacts and displays, not to mention a world-class collection of jasper, agates, and other gems donated by a pair of rockhounding locals.

2 Baldwin Hotel Museum

31 Main St., Klamath Falls 97601; (541) 882-1000
klamathcountymuseum.squarespace.com/visitthemuseum

Built in 1905, the Baldwin Hotel is an impressive sight, and it took in guests for nearly 70 years before eventually being converted to a museum. While most museums focus on a particular aspect of area history, the Baldwin Museum's varied, interesting collections essentially allow it to serve as several museums in one. Of course, there are restored rooms that show what life was like in the hotel, but there are also exhibits and artifacts pertaining to domestic life, healthcare, photography, and more. *Note:* The museum closes in the winter, so plan accordingly.

3 Coos Art Museum

235 Anderson Ave., Coos Bay 97420; (541) 267-3901
coosart.org

The art scene in Coos Bay has been thriving for decades, but the process of finding a suitable museum site was something of a Herculean effort. The museum's first home was the town's old Carnegie Library.

After the successful passage of a city bond and years-long renovations, the museum opened its doors in its present location: the town's Art Deco–style post office. Today, the museum has three galleries and more than 500 pieces in its permanent collections; it also offers art classes, workshops, and special exhibits and shows.

4 Fort Dalles Museum

500 W. 15th St., The Dalles 97058; (541) 296-4547
fortdallesmuseum.org

As its name suggests, Fort Dalles was once a military base; its troops were active in the Yakima War, when the fort was known as Fort Drum. The Yakima War ended in 1858, and less than a decade later, the fort was abandoned after a fire destroyed the officers' quarters. Today, it is a museum, and one of its primary buildings was constructed as the surgeon's quarters for the original base. It's filled with artifacts from the military history of the time, as well as tools, buildings, old vehicles, and an intact homestead that dates back to 1895. The museum is also home to demonstrations about pioneer life, concerts, lectures, and more.

5 High Desert Museum

59800 US 97, Bend 97702; (541) 382-4754
highdesertmuseum.org

There's so much on offer at the High Desert Museum that it's hard to know where to start. It has more than 100,000 square feet of exhibit space (both indoors and out), with 11 permanent exhibits about the history, wildlife, and cultures of the region, not to mention a slate of temporary exhibits each year. The museum also has a number of resident animals, from Gila monsters and rattlesnakes in its Desertarium to otters, porcupines, and rescued raptors and birds of prey, not to mention the wild critters you might spot out on the museum's nature trails. The museum also has an impressive collection of items pertaining to the many cultures and peoples of the region. Its collections include an authentic stagecoach and other items from the pioneer era, items detailing the many contributions of Chinese immigrants to the region, and many Native American artifacts and works of art.

6 Maude Kerns Art Center

1910 E. 15th Ave., Eugene 97403; (541) 345-1571
mkartcenter.org

Maude Kerns's "nonobjective" art is a little hard to describe. These abstract works consist largely of geometric forms such as circles and rectangles, and they aren't intended to depict or represent an object

(say, as in a landscape). Instead, composition and arrangement are paramount, and simple representation is beside the point. Kerns was an important player in the nonobjective-art movement, and her work is now found in the permanent collection of major art galleries around the country. The community arts center that bears her name now offers exhibits, classes, and special events, and it's home to more than 70 pieces produced by Kerns in her career.

7 Oregon State Hospital Museum of Mental Health

2600 Center St. NE, Salem 97301; (971) 599-1674
oshmuseum.org

Located on the grounds of the Oregon State Hospital (which is still in operation), this museum is unlike any other you'll encounter in Oregon. Housed in the oldest building on campus, the 2,500-square-foot museum provides an inside look at what life was like at this hospital—both for workers and for patients—over the past century. The museum has something of an interactive feel: at the visitor center, you're given an ID badge with the name of a patient or staff member, and as you proceed through the museum, you can look for more information about that person's life and story. Along the way, you'll see exhibits and artifacts that tell the complicated human stories that have unfolded here. There's even a restored ward room where you can see up close what life was like as a patient. And if the museum seems eerily familiar, there's a good reason for that: it's also famous as the filming location for *One Flew Over the Cuckoo's Nest*.

8 Portland Art Museum

1219 SW Park Ave., Portland 97205; (503) 226-2811
portlandartmuseum.org

Founded in 1892, the Portland Art Museum is the oldest art museum in the Pacific Northwest and one of the oldest in the country. Today, the sprawling museum has more than 110,000 feet of gallery space and tens of thousands of works in its collection, and it is home to major traveling exhibits as well. The collections include more than

3,500 pieces of Native American art; an expansive collection by artists with ties to the Pacific Northwest; and a world-class lineup of American, Asian, and European art.

9 Rice Northwest Museum of Rocks and Minerals

26385 NW Groveland Drive, Hillsboro 97124; (503) 647-2418
ricenorthwestmuseum.org

It's hard to know what's more of draw at this museum: its top-flight collection of some 20,000 rocks and minerals, with more than 4,000 on display, or the building it's housed in: a midcentury ranch-style house that is now listed on the National Register of Historic Places. Helen and Richard Rice built this remarkable home in the 1950s, and they soon dedicated a room in it to their growing rock and mineral collection. The entire house became museum space in the 1990s, with another building added on soon thereafter. With thunder eggs, agates, meteorites, and more, it's now a major draw for rockhounds and architecture buffs alike.

Chinese lanterns hang above Fred Meyer Plaza at the front entrance of the Portland Art Museum.

On the Wildwood Trail in Forest Park, Portland

IT ALMOST GOES without saying that Oregon is paradise when it comes to nature and the outdoors. Whether you're interested in beaches and tide pools (page 56), wild rivers, the high desert, or deep forests and mountain lakes, Oregon has it. The hardest decision is usually a good problem: what to do first.

OUTDOOR ADVENTURES

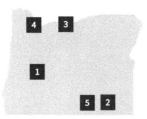

1 Alpine Trail #3450

Willamette National Forest Middle Fork Ranger District, Westfir 97492;
(541) 782-2283
Starting trailhead: Forest Service Road 5821 (2.7 miles north of OR 58), Westfir
97492; GPS: 43.76090, -122.52200
Ending trailhead: Intersection of Forest Service Roads 1912 and 1825, Oakridge
97463; GPS: 43.90113, -122.46535; mtbproject.com/trail/4324612/alpine-3450,
tinyurl.com/alpinetrail3450

There are more than a few mountain biking trails in Oregon, but
the 15-mile-long Alpine Trail is consistently ranked among the best
singletrack trails in the state. The reason is simple: it's absolutely
stunning. Mostly downhill, there are convenient shuttles (you'll need
to pay for them) that spare you the trouble of slogging all the way
up the mountain, and the scenery is so good that the trail is often
known simply as "The Jedi," for its resemblance to the forests from
Star Wars: Episode VI—Return of the Jedi. Before you head out, make
sure you've got a few trails under your belt and a suitable bike, and
familiarize yourself with the shuttle options and the route's actual
twists and turns. Also, note that the trail is shared with hikers and
horses, so please bike carefully and considerately.

2 Alvord Desert

Alvord Hot Springs Access 36095 E. Steens Road (Fields–Denio Road), Princeton,
OR 97721; GPS: 42.54464, -118.53038; (541) 589-2282
alvordhotsprings.com (or Google "Alvord Desert" for a multitude of helpful articles)

Around a dozen miles long and maybe half as wide, the Alvord
Desert is a dried lakebed that looks like something out of a science
fiction film. It certainly seems out of place for Oregon, and that's
part of what makes it delightful. It's wonderfully remote, serene,
and beautiful, with almost perfectly dark night skies. When the
weather is right, it's a great spot to camp, stargaze, or take in
nearby hot springs. But before you head out, be sure to plan ahead.
For obvious reasons, the dry season (late summer–fall) is often best,
so if you want to see the desert for yourself, you'll want to check the
latest forecasts.

Make no mistake: this is a remote area, and cell reception and services aren't always available, so fill up your gas tank in one of the two closest towns (Burns to the north or Fields to the south), and bring extra water, food, a map, atlas, and/or dedicated GPS unit just in case. Also, this being a desert and all, there's no address to speak of. Most online articles recommend using Alvord Hot Springs as a base for exploring. They do charge a fee to use their access road—happily, that also gives you access to their heavenly soaking pools (and they waive the use fee if you camp in their facilities).

3 Deschutes River State Recreation Area

89600 Biggs–Rufus Highway (OR 206), Wasco 97065, (541) 739-2322
tinyurl.com/deschutesriversra

The canyons rising above the Deschutes River keep temperatures warmer than you might expect in spring. When many places in Oregon are still sprinkled with snow, flowers start to bloom as early as February in this state park. In spring and summer, the park offers everything from dedicated hiking and mountain biking trails to camping, river rapids, and fly-fishing from shore (no bait is allowed). Reservations or boating passes are required, so check in advance for information.

4 Forest Park

Bounded by West Burnside Road to the south, NW Mount St. Helens Road (US 30) to the east, NW Skyline Boulevard to the west, and NW Newberry Road to the north, Northwest Portland; (503) 823-7529, (503) 223-5449
portland.gov/parks/forest-park, forestparkconservancy.org/forest-park

In almost any other city, Forest Park would have been clear-cut to build houses or warehouses long ago. But in Portland, Forest Park is just that: a sprawling, miles-long urban forest in shouting distance from downtown. Preserved due to a combination of natural good fortune—the underlying geology isn't ideal for construction—and several generations of forward-thinking town leaders, it's now a wild, green space packed with hiking and biking trails and wildlife, and it's an easy place to escape from civilization. The park is open every day from 5 a.m. to 10 p.m. The two websites above have all the maps and information you'll need to plan the perfect day here.

5 Hart Mountain Springs

Hart Mountain National Antelope Refuge 38782 Hart Mountain Road (County Road 3-12), Plush 97637; GPS: 42.46157, -119.80575; (541) 947-2731
fws.gov/refuge/hart_mountain

When you think of a national wildlife refuge, especially one that's seemingly in the wilderness, you might not think of a relaxing hot spring. But lo and behold, if you visit the Hart Mountain National

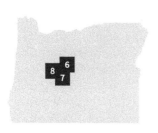

Antelope Refuge, located near Plush, Oregon, you'll find wildlife, gorgeous scenery, solitude, and yes, a hot springs. Collected in a pool-like structure, the spring water stays a toasty 100°F–105°F. (There's another "undeveloped" pool nearby to try out too.) Before you visit, it's highly recommended that you plan ahead, as the refuge is remote and services and road access aren't always available, especially in winter. As part of your planning, be sure to download the printable PDF with detailed driving directions (including where to stop for gas and food) from points north, south, and in between.

6 Smith Rock State Park

NE Crooked River Drive (3.2 miles east of US 97), Terrebonne 97760; GPS: 44.36432, -121.13892; (541) 548-7501
tinyurl.com/smithrockstatepark

Known as "The Birthplace of U.S. Sport Climbing," or climbing that relies on permanent anchors, this state park has more than 2,000 climbing routes. It's also a destination for other adventurous fun, such as slacklining, with more than 30 routes in all. (Slacklining is essentially moving across an anchored stretch of nylon webbing, sort of similar to walking a tightrope.) Located about 27 miles northeast of Bend, Smith Rock State Park is unique in that you can slackline among the geological features in the park. You'll have to see this "high line" slacklining to believe it, but it has a solid safety record thanks to redundant safety equipment, harnesses, and so on. For those who want to stay on solid ground, there are plenty of hiking options, including everything from family-friendly hikes to ones with foreboding names like Misery Ridge.

7 Sunriver Resort

17600 Center Drive, Sunriver 97707; (855) 420-8206
sunriverresort.com

Golfers, rejoice: Sunriver features four golf courses. Two are public courses, and two are open only to club members or resort guests. Novices and families can start at the Links at Caldera, a private 9-hole course perfect for families and beginners. The nationally recognized Crosswater, also a private course, is 18 holes and intended for serious golfers and the adventurous. Winding through the wilderness, golfers will encounter wetlands, rivers, and woodlands. Two Sunriver courses, Meadows and Woodlands, are open to the public. If golfing isn't your thing, the resort offers dining options and a spa; the Sunriver Nature Center and the Oregon Observatory are also nearby.

8 Three Sisters Wilderness

Deschutes National Forest Bend–Fort Rock Ranger District, Bend 97701; Sisters Ranger District, Sisters 97759; (541) 383-5300, (541) 549-7700
Willamette National Forest McKenzie River Ranger District, McKenzie Bridge 97413; (541) 822-3381
tinyurl.com/threesisterswilderness

The Three Sisters Wilderness gets its name from a towering trio of stratovolcanoes, known as the South Sister, the Middle Sister, and the North Sister. All three are around the same height (just over 10,000 feet), but they differ in terms of their composition and age. Today, the wilderness area covers more than 280,000 acres and offers hundreds of miles of trails, including a long section of the Pacific Crest Trail. The views here are absolutely stunning and the land pristine, but if you visit, keep in mind that this area is a true wilderness—there are no facilities—so you'll need to plan accordingly. You'll also need a wilderness permit; check the website above for details before you go. Finally, you'll need to take along at least one high-quality map, as this is a vast expanse of land spanning two national forests. We recommend Adventure Maps' *Three Sisters Wilderness Trail Map* (adventuremaps.net) and National Geographic Maps' *818–Bend Three Sisters Map* (natgeomaps.com).

Smith Rock State Park

All aboard the Candy Cane Express at the Oregon Rail Heritage Center!

OREGON HAS RAILROADS COVERED. Learn about the heritage of the state's trains through museums, exhibits, and, of course, riding the rails on a vintage train. These family-friendly adventures offer fun, scenery, and an unforgettable experience.

RAILROADS

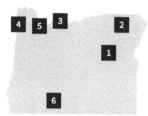

1 DeWitt Museum

Depot Park Main and Bridge Streets, Prairie City 97869; (541) 820-3330
prairiecityoregon.com/prairie-city-oregon-dewitt-museum.html

If you want to get a sense of what it was like to ride the rails in the
early 20th century, head here. This preserved two-story depot is
included on the National Register of Historic Places. Railway service
stopped here in 1933, and the building was a residence until it was
preserved by forward-thinking community members. Today, it's
brimming with interesting artifacts pertaining to railway history,
rocks and minerals, and photographs that provide a window into
the railway during its halcyon days. The museum is open May 15–
October 15, Wednesday–Sunday, 10 a.m.–5 p.m.

2 Eagle Cap Train Rides

Elgin Depot 300 Depot St., Elgin 97827; (541) 437-3652
eaglecaptrainrides.com

This round-trip train ride starts at the Elgin Depot, built to resemble
the historic depot that once stood here. There you'll find a ticket
office, a gift shop, and historical relics from the railroad's earlier
days. The route travels just under 40 miles and takes about 4 hours,
with food and drinks usually included. If you're traveling with a
group, you can reserve an entire train car or, if you have a special
event in mind, even the entire train.

3 Mount Hood Railway

110 Railroad St., Hood River 97031; (541) 399-8939
mthoodrr.com

Hop aboard a century-old railway on a scenic excursion through the
Columbia River Gorge. The train station is located in Hood River, and
the scenery here is supreme: Mt. Hood towers majestically in the distance, and the train tracks pass by wild rivers and through orchards,
vineyards, and forests. The locomotive stops in Parkdale, where
lunch is available at the Hutson Museum, which has an impressive
rock collection and a variety of other interesting items. Depending
on the season, there are also themed train rides, including Christmas
rides, and more.

4 Oregon Coast Scenic Railroad

306 American Ave., Garibaldi 97718; (503) 842-7972
oregoncoastscenic.org

Relax in comfort on a steam locomotive while the Pacific Coast rolls by. This scenic, hour-and-a-half-long route travels between Rockaway Beach and Garibaldi during the summer months; seasonal special events are also available, such as Fourth of July rides, trips to enjoy the fall colors, and the Candy Cane Express. The train rides are guided and interpreted by the railroad's knowledgeable staff members. Perhaps best of all, this scenic railroad is environmentally friendly, recycling used motor oil to run its trains.

5 Oregon Rail Heritage Center

2250 SE Water Ave., Portland 97214; (503) 233-1156
orhf.org

This amazing facility is unlike many other museums dedicated to transportation history: two of the three steam engines preserved here are actually operational, and a third is currently being restored. Bringing these locomotives back to life has been a herculean effort—overseen by an all-volunteer crew. Reviving these magnificent machines—the center's Southern Pacific 4449 is simply gorgeous—was no small feat, given that the site's youngest locomotive was built in 1941, with the oldest built in 1905. Many of the parts and components for the engines had to be built from scratch; this is why the center maintains an active machine shop on-site. Don't miss the center during the holiday season: its Holiday Train is a beautiful sight and has become a winter tradition. One of the center's steam engines pulls vintage rail cars covered in Christmas lights along the Willamette River and into Portland. If you're lucky enough to snag a ticket—they go on sale in July—you can join the fun!

Note: The center has somewhat limited hours, so check its website before you visit.

6 Train Mountain Railroad Museum

36941 S. Chiloquin Road, Chiloquin 97624; (541) 783-3030
trainmountain.org

This is a rail fan's paradise. Home to the world's largest miniature railroad (37 miles of 7.5 gauge track) and spanning a whopping 2,200 acres, this place has it all: train rides; 37 different full-size train cabooses; and a wide variety of rolling stock, including snow-removal cars, those with ties to the logging industry, and flat cars. The nonprofit museum's dedicated volunteers also offer occasional lectures and programs and maintain a railway library.

Dug Bar and its historical monument

NATIVE AMERICAN CULTURE

HISTORICAL, EDUCATIONAL & RECREATIONAL SITES

Cascadia Cave

Willamette National Forest North side of US 20 in Cascadia, about 60 miles northeast of Eugene; GPS: 44.39890, -122.45720; (541) 367-5168, (877) 444-6777; recreation.gov/ticket/233373/ticket/21

Discovered in the 1930s, Cascadia Cave contains petroglyphs believed to have been created by the Kalapuya and Molalla peoples around 8,000 years ago. Cave tours are held just twice a year—once in June and again in September (book at the website above).

Dug Bar

Nez Perce National Historical Park/Wallowa-Whitman National Forest
Forest Road 4260, 31 miles north of Imnaha, just across the Snake River from Idaho; GPS: 45.80460, -116.68670; (208) 843-7001
nps.gov/nepe/planyourvisit/visit-dug-bar.htm, tinyurl.com/dugbartrailhead

Dug Bar marks the spot where, in 1877, Chief Joseph and the Nez Perce tribe forded the Snake River while being forcibly relocated from their Oregon homeland to a reservation in Idaho. Today it serves not only as a historic site but also as a boat launch and a starting point for several hiking trails in Wallowa-Whitman National Forest.

Sherars Falls

OR 216 (Sherars Bridge Highway), about 38 miles south of The Dalles; GPS: 45.26361, -121.03240; (541) 553-3557
fisheries.warmsprings-nsn.gov/permits/sherars-falls-access-permit-day-use-2

This long-standing tribal fishing area on the Deschutes River is managed by the Confederated Tribes of Warm Springs. Access requires buying a permit at the website above.

MUSEUMS

Tamástslikt Cultural Institute
Confederated Tribes of the Umatilla Indian Reservation
47106 Wildhorse Blvd., Pendleton 97801; (541) 429-7700
tamastslikt.org

Chachalu Tribal Museum and Cultural Center
Confederated Tribes of Grand Ronde 9615 Grand Ronde Road, Grand Ronde 97347; (503) 879-5211
grandronde.org/history-culture/culture/chachalu-museum-and-cultural-center

The Museum at Warm Springs
Confederated Tribes of Warm Springs 2189 OR 26, Warm Springs 97761; (541) 553-3331
museumatwarmsprings.org

POWWOWS

Note: Due to the pandemic, many annual powwows in Oregon have not yet been announced for 2021 at the time of this writing; the following listings generally indicate when the powwows took place prior to 2020 and assume that they will resume at some point in the near future. For the latest information and updates, check the websites below or check the event calendar at powwows. com (on the homepage, choose "Calendar," then click "Pow Wows by State," then click "Oregon").

Annual Contest Powwow
Confederated Tribes of Grand Ronde Willamina, August
grandronde.org/events

Native American Arts Festival & Mother's Day Powwow
Grants Pass, May facebook.com/nativeartsfestival

Nesika Illahee Pow-Wow
Confederated Tribes of Siletz Indians Siletz, August
ctsi.nsn.us/chinook-indian-tribe-siletz-heritage/pow-wow/schedule-of-events

Northern Paiute Powwow & Lacrosse Games
Burns Paiute Tribe Burns, August
burnspaiute-nsn.gov, facebook.com/paiute2020

Oregon State University Klatowa Eena Powwow
Corvallis, May dce.oregonstate.edu/pow-wow-information

Pi-Ume-Sha Treaty Days Pow Wow Celebration
Confederated Tribes of Warm Springs Warm Springs, June
warmsprings-nsn.gov/events

Powwow at La Pine
The Klamath Tribes (Klamath, Modoc, Yahooskin) La Pine, October
klamathtribes.org

Tamkaliks Celebration and Friendship Feast
Nez Perce Wallowa Homeland Wallowa, July
wallowanezperce.org/tamkaliks

University of Oregon Native American Student Union Mother's Day Pow-Wow
Eugene, May facebook.com/uo.nasu

Western Oregon University Multicultural Student Union Pow-Wow
Monmouth, April wou.edu/msu/annual-programs/pow-wow

Wildhorse Pow Wow
Confederated Tribes of the Umatilla Indian Reservation Pendleton, July
wildhorseresort.com/entertainment/events

Willamette University Native and Indigenous Student Union Social Powwow
Salem, March willamette.edu/offices/oma/events/powwow

Applegate Valley winery near Ashland, Oregon

VINEYARDS, FRUIT, & MORE

If you like wine, you've come to the right state. Thanks to its climate and ideal soils, Oregon has more than 700 different wineries. Obviously, listing them individually would be a book-length effort, so consider this section as the briefest of introductions to Oregon wines and wineries. In addition to wines, Oregon also boasts plenty of you-pick farms, farms open for visits, distilleries, and more. The list below focuses primarily on wineries and such, but check out the websites listed below for other fun stops!

CANBY FARM LOOP
(Makes 10 stops in the Canby-Aurora area just south of Portland)
canbyfarmloop.com

Christopher Bridge Wines
12770 S. Casto Rd., Oregon City
http://christopherbridgewines.com

Fir Point Farms
firpointfarms.com
14601 Arndt Rd., Aurora

King's Raven Winery
11603 S. New Era Rd., Oregon City
kingsravenwine.com

Villa Catalana Cellars
11900 S. Criteser Rd., Oregon City
https://villacatalanacellars.com

DUNDEE WINERIES
(Directory of 37 wineries in the Dundee area)
traveldundeeoregon.com/wineries

Argyle Winery
691 Hwy 99W, Dundee
https://argylewinery.com

(continued on next page)

Bella Vida
9380 NE Worden Hill Rd., Dundee
https://bellavida.com

Duck Pond Cellars
23145 Hwy 99W, Dundee
https://www.greatoregonwine.com

Hawkins Cellars
990 Hwy 99W, Dundee
https://hawkinscellars.com

Sokol Blosser
5000 Sokol Blosser Ln., Dundee
https://sokolblosser.com

HOOD RIVER FRUIT LOOP
(Makes 26 stops in and around Hood River)
hoodriverfruitloop.com

Cathedral Ridge Winery
4200 Post Canyon Dr, Hood River
cathedralridgewinery.com

Draper Girls Cider Company
6200 Hwy 35, Parkdale
drapergirlscider.com

Fox-Tail Cider & Distillery
2965 Ehrck Hill Road #2, Hood River
foxtailcider.com

Grateful Vineyard
6670 Trout Creek Ridge Rd., Mt. Hood
gratefulvineyards.com

Hood Crest Winery and Distillers
1900 Orchard Rd., Hood River
hoodcrestwinery.com

Marchesi Vineyard
3955 Belmont Dr., Hood River
marchesivineyards.com

Mt. Hood Winery
2882 Van Horn Dr., Hood River

Mt. View Orchards and Cidery
6670 Trout Creek Rdige Rd., Mt. Hood
mtvieworchards.com

Phelps Creek Vineyards
1850 Country Club Road, Hood River
phelpscreekvineyards.com

Stave & Stone Winery
3827 Fletcher Dr., Hood River
https://staveandstone.com/

MOLALLA COUNTRY FARM LOOP
(Makes 12 stops in the Molalla area south of Portland; located directly south of the Canby Farm Loop, above)
molallafarmloop.com

Forest Edge Vineyard
15640 S Spangler Rd., Oregon City
forestedgevineyard.com

SAUVIE ISLAND
(An island in the Columbia River that's chock-full of farm stands, U-pick farms, and plant nurseries)
sauvieisland.org

SOUTHERN OREGON WINERY ASSOCIATION
(Listings for many member wineries); southernoregonwine.org

There are far too many wineries to list individually here; in fact, the Southern Oregon Winery Association divides the area into region. See their website for more details

A Mt. Hood-area winery

At the Wooden Shoe Tulip Fest

NOTE: DUE TO THE PANDEMIC, some festivals have not yet been announced at the time of this writing. Check the websites below for the latest information.

FESTIVALS

MOUNT ANGEL OKTOBERFEST
Mount Angel late September
oktoberfest.org

PENDLETON ROUND-UP
Pendleton September
pendletonroundup.com

PORTLAND GREEK FESTIVAL
Portland October
portlandgreekfestival.com, facebook.com/portlandgreekfestival

PORTLAND HIGHLAND GAMES
Gresham July (*note:* postponed until 2022)
phga.org

PORTLAND ROSE FESTIVAL
Portland late May–early June (*note:* postponed until 2022, with some smaller events taking place in 2021; see website for details)
rosefestival.org

SHREWSBURY RENAISSANCE FAIRE
Kings Valley September shrewfaire.com

SOUTHERN OREGON KITE FESTIVAL
Brookings July
southernoregonkitefestival.com

WOODEN SHOE TULIP FEST
Woodburn early March–early May
woodenshoe.com/events/tulip-fest

Oregon State's Reser Stadium

SPORTS

PORTLAND TRAILBLAZERS, NATIONAL BASKETBALL ASSOCIATION
Moda Center, 1 N Center Court St., Portland, OR 97227
www.nba.com/blazers

PORTLAND TIMBERS, MAJOR LEAGUE SOCCER
Providence Park, 1844 SW Morrison St., Portland, OR 97205
www.timbers.com

PORTLAND THORNS FC, NATIONAL WOMEN'S SOCCER LEAGUE
Providence Park, 1844 SW Morrison St., Portland, OR 97205
www.timbers.com/thornsfc

HILLSBORO HOPS, MINOR LEAGUE BASEBALL
Ron Tonkin Field, 4460 NE Century Blvd., Hillsboro, OR 97124
www.milb.com/hillsboro

PORTLAND PICKLES, WEST COAST LEAGUE
Walker Stadium, 4727 SE 92nd Ave., Portland, OR, 97266
www.portlandpicklesbaseball.com

PORTLAND WINTERHAWKS, WESTERN HOCKEY LEAGUE
Moda Center or Veterans Memorial Coliseum, both in Portland
https://winterhawks.com/

**ROSE CITY ROLLERS, WOMEN'S FLAT TRACK DERBY ASSOCIATION
(roller derby)**
The Hangar at Oaks Amusement Park, 7805 SE Oaks Park Way
www.rosecityrollers.com

UNIVERSITY OF OREGON (DUCKS, MULTIPLE SPORTS)
https://goducks.com/

OREGON STATE UNIVERSITY (Beavers, multiple sports)
https://osubeavers.com/

UNIVERSITY OF PORTLAND (Pilots, multiple sports)
https://portlandpilots.com/

PORTLAND STATE UNIVERSITY (Vikings)
https://goviks.com/

Mt. Hood seen from Trillium Lake, Oregon

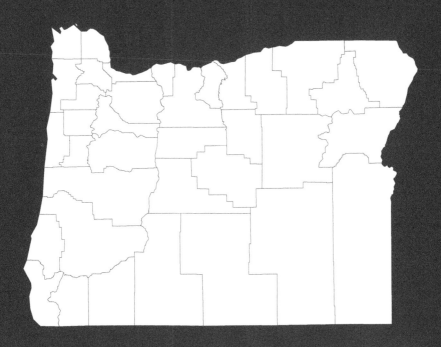

OREGON STATE
Symbols, Emblems, & Trivia

COUNTIES: 36 **POPULATION, PER THE US CENSUS: 4,217,737**
FOUNDING AS US STATE: February 14, 1859 *(33rd state to enter the Union)*

State Flag

Oregon's navy-blue-and-gold state flag features the state seal on one side, along with 33 stars (a nod to its status as the 33rd state to enter the Union). The seal itself features an eagle, mountains, elk, a settler's wagon, a farmer's plough, a sheaf of wheat, and a miner's pickaxe. The flag also shows the Pacific Coast with two ships: a British Navy vessel departing, and a US merchant vessel arriving. Oregon's flag is also notable for something downright odd: It has two sides. The other side features a beaver, long an icon of Oregon and the Pacific Northwest.

STATE FLOWER: Oregon Grape
(Mahonia aquifolium)

Despite its common name, Oregon Grape actually belongs to the barberry family, though you wouldn't know it from a quick glance at its dark blue fruit, which really does resemble a miniature bunch of grapes. Its bright-yellow flowers precede the berries, and they appear in groups. The edible berries don't taste much like grapes but are used in jam and country wines.

STATE TREE: Douglas-fir *(Pseudotsuga menziesii)*

An iconic tree of the Pacific Northwest, the Douglas-fir can reach well over 200 feet in height; the record tree in Oregon, found in Coos County, reaches an amazing 329 feet. But even average trees are often towering and impressive. An important tree for the lumber industry, and a popular choice as a landscaping tree, the Douglas-fir's common name is a nod to Scottish Botanist Douglas, who helped popularize the tree and introduced it to cultivation. The Douglas-fir may be most familiar as a Christmas tree; it's one of the most popular Christmas tree options nationwide.

STATE FISH: Chinook Salmon *(Oncorhynchus tshawytscha)*

Chinook Salmon are large salmon—average fish can reach 3 feet long—and some spectacular specimens can reach perhaps 5 feet. (Oregon's state record fish was 83 pounds!) Chinook Salmon are anadromous, which means they are born in rivers, but then head to the ocean, where they reach maturity after several years. Once they are capable of breeding, they migrate all the way back to their birthplace, where they spawn, and then die. This lifecycle makes salmon especially susceptible to dam construction, pollution, and the like, and it also makes them important species in both their spawning grounds and in the open ocean.

STATE BIRD: Western Meadowlark
(Sturnella neglecta)

Spotting this bird can be tricky at times, but its beautiful call is familiar across Oregon. Found in prairies and fields, these birds primarily eat insects and other "bugs," including grasshoppers, beetles, and spiders. They also feed upon seeds in farm fields and may venture to seed feeders.

STATE ANIMAL:
Beaver
(Castor canadensis)

Oregon's state mammal, the beaver is found in rivers and streams through-out Oregon. Long hunted for its fine pelt, beavers were nearly extirpated from Oregon when settlers and colonists hunted them nearly to extinction. Beaver pelts were in high demand in Europe, due in part to a fashion craze for beaver-pelt hats, and Oregon became a hot spot for the beaver trade, earning Oregon its nickname of the "Beaver State." Happily, beaver populations have since largely recovered.

STATE INSECT: Oregon Swallowtail Butterfly
(Papilio machaon oregonius)

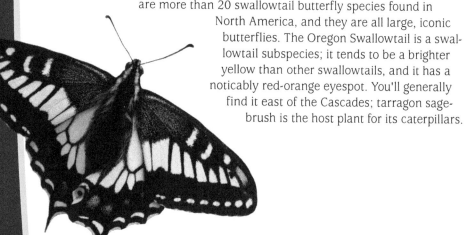

These large, fast butterflies are named for their hindwing tails, which resemble the forked tails found in many swallow species. There are more than 20 swallowtail butterfly species found in North America, and they are all large, iconic butterflies. The Oregon Swallowtail is a swallowtail subspecies; it tends to be a brighter yellow than other swallowtails, and it has a noticably red-orange eyespot. You'll generally find it east of the Cascades; tarragon sagebrush is the host plant for its caterpillars.

STATE FOSSIL: Metasequoia

This redwood tree was once found in prehistoric Oregon, and fossils of its leaves are relatively common. It lived during the Miocene (around 23-5 million years ago). Long thought extinct, living specimens of the tree were identified in China in the 1940s, and today, living specimens of the tree (gifts from some of the original researchers) can now be found on the campus of Oregon State University.

STATE MUSHROOM:
Pacific Golden
Chanterelle
(Cantharellus formosus)

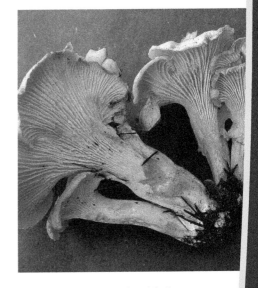

Prized by foragers and chefs alike, the Pacific Golden Chanterelle is a bright-yellow mushroom that has a mutually beneficial relationship with certain trees, notably western hemlock and other conifers. Found from fall through winter, the chanterelle is a large, showy mushroom with a long stem and false gills. Mycologists haven't found a reliable way to cultivate them yet, but thankfully chanterelles often appear in groups, making it easy to harvest a number at a time. Note: Don't use the description here to identify chanterelles; instead, join a mushroom-hunting club, purchase field guides, and be sure of your identification before consuming any wild mushrooms.

STATE GEMSTONE:
Oregon Sunstone

Oregon Sunstone is found only in Oregon. A type of the mineral feldspar, known as labradorite. Oregon's sunstone is known for its wonderful colors, from clear and pink specimens to deep reds and greens. Some finds exhibit what's known as a "schiller" or "labradorescence," a beautiful play of light caused by diffraction from layers within the stone. Sunstone is rare, but it can be collected from Bureau of Land Management land in southern Oregon. For details, visit: www.blm.gov/visit/sunstone -collection-area

STATE ROCK: Thunderegg

On the outside, Thundereggs don't usually look like much: a bumpy, brown, mostly oval lump of rock. They formed when lava or volcanic ash solidified into rock, and the gas inside it created pockets where mineral-rich water filled in and hardened. That means that if you cut open a Thunderegg, the drab exterior gives way to a beautiful, often colorful interior. This makes Thundereggs incredibly collectible, fun to find, and sometimes valuable. You can hunt for them yourselves at pay-to-dig mines, or you can often find them in gift shops or online. However you get one, they are a wonderful keepsake.

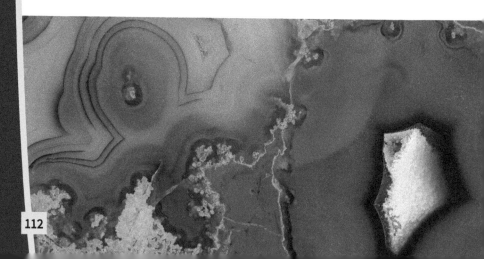

STATE SEASHELL: Oregon Hairy Triton

Difficult to find, but stunning, this "hairy" seashell is found along much of the Pacific Coast, but often in deep water. Reaching 3-5 inches in length, this large snail is a predator on a variety of other organisms, including sea stars, urchins, and others.

STATE MICROBE:
Saccharomyces cerevisiae

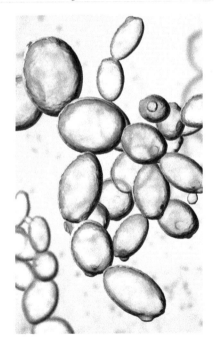

A rarity among state symbols, Oregon has a state microbe. While the scientific name might not ring a bell, the end product it helps make is a familiar one in Oregon and the wider Pacific Northwest: beer. Oregon is a craft brewing paradise and *Saccharomyces cerevisiae* is the organism that makes it possible. Yeast are single-celled fungi, and they produce the alcohol and carbon dioxide found in beer. (The same types of yeast are used in breadmaking.)

DEEPEST LAKE: Crater Lake (1,943 feet deep)

The deepest lake in the United States, and one of the top 10 deepest in the world, Crater Lake is aptly named, as it occupies part of the crater of an active volcanic complex. More than a third of a mile deep, the lake is also situated at a lofty elevation, more than 6,000 feet above sea level. Still, its deep blue waters, the stunning surroundings of the national park that encompass it, and the allure of standing next to, well, a volcano, draw folks from all over.

Note: Because the lake is situated high in the mountains, snow persists well into spring/summer, so always check in advance about road closures, icy conditions, and general accessibility concerns: www.nps.gov/crla/index.htm.

HIGHEST WATERFALL: Multnomah Falls (620 feet)

As popular as it is tall, Multnomah Falls is located just under an hour east of Portland. The waterfall actually consists of two falls, and there is a scenic bridge in between them, which provides a wonderful view of the much-taller upper falls. The falls are often most impressive in spring and fall. Note: The site sees a huge number of tourists each year, so there's plenty to do in the wider Columbia River Gorge area.

TALLEST MOUNTAIN: Mt. Hood (11,250 feet)

Located just about 50 miles east of Portland, Mt. Hood is the tallest mountain in the state. It's also an active volcano, and the United States Geological Survey (USGS) considers it one of the greater volcanic threats in the country, in large part because an eruption could produce lahars (volcanic mudflows) or other potential hazards. Thankfully, the USGS is carefully monitoring Mt. Hood and the many other volcanoes in Oregon and the Pacific Region, so don't let its volcanic status dissuade you from heading out to the Mt. Hood area (or the Mt. Hood National Forest) for the amazing hiking, camping, and sightseeing in the mountain's vicinity.

The Three Sisters Mountains near Sisters, Oregon

Picturesque Oregon: Waterfalls

Descriptions of Oregon hardly do its beauty justice, especially when it comes to its hundreds of waterfalls. From massive falls that plummet hundreds of feet to ephemeral waterfalls that appear with rainfall, only to disappear soon after, Oregon's waterfalls are always people-pleasers. Here's a look at a few of those mentioned earlier in the book.

Multnomah Falls (page 13)

Drift Creek Falls (page 12)

White River Falls (page 15)

Koosah Falls (page 14)

Munson Creek Falls (page 13)

Watson Falls (page 14)

Hug Point Falls (page 13)

Sweet Creek Falls (page 14)

Picturesque Oregon: Beaches and Sea Stacks

From beaches with huge sea stacks looming just offshore to rock-strewn beaches with agates, jade, and other potential finds underfoot, Oregon's beaches have a lot to offer, both in terms of their scenery and a host of fun things to do.

Cannon Beach (page 58)

Depoe Bay (page 59)

Gold Beach (page 59)

Ghost Forest on Neskowin Beach (page 60)

Port Orford (page 60)

Rockaway Beach (page 61)

Peter Iredale Shipwreck (page 66)

Arch Cape (page 61)

Picturesque Oregon: Lighthouses

With its huge expanses of coastline, treacherous offshore reefs and currents, and a myriad of merchant vessels plying its waters for much of its recent history, it's probably not surprising that Oregon is home to more than a few wrecks. In response, a number of lighthouses were built to help guide sailors to a safe harbor.

Cape Meares Lighthouse (page 46)

Umpqua Lighthouse (page 48)

Cape Blanco State Park (page 46)

Tillamook Rock Lighthouse (page 47)

Yaquina Bay Lighthouse (page 48)

Coquille River Lighthouse (page 47)

Index

OREGON

YOUR CAR-CAMPING GUIDE TO SCENIC BEAUTY, THE SOUNDS
OF NATURE, AND AN ESCAPE FROM CIVILIZATION

*FIND OREGON'S
BEST
CAMPSITES!*

Best Tent Camping: Oregon

Becky Ohlsen

**ISBN: 978-0-89732-677-3 • $16.95 • 6 x 9 • paperback
192 pages • full-color photos**

Oregon provides a spectacular backdrop for some of the most scenic campgrounds in the country. But do you know which campgrounds offer the most privacy? Which are the best for first-time campers? Becky Ohlsen traversed the entire state and compiled the most up-to-date research to steer you to the perfect spot! Best Tent Camping: Oregon presents 50 campgrounds. Selections are based on location, topography, size, and overall appeal, and every site is rated for beauty, privacy, spaciousness, safety and security, and cleanliness so you'll always know what to expect.

STAN TEKIELA's

Birding for Beginners

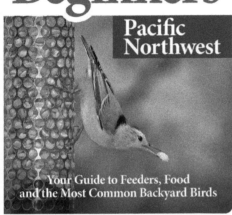

Pacific Northwest

Your Guide to Feeders, Food
and the Most Common Backyard Birds

*FIND JOY IN
THE WONDER
OF BIRDS*

Birding for Beginners: Pacific Northwest

Stan Tekiela

ISBN: 978-1-64755-121-6 • $16.95 • 5.25 x 7.25 • paperback •
176 pages • full-color photos

Award-winning author, naturalist, and wildlife photographer
Stan Tekiela provides the information you need to become a
birder. Learn the basics of bird feeders. Create a bird-friendly
yard and even make your own bird food. The book is also an
identification guide, featuring 57 birds that are most likely to
be found near your area. The species are organized by color,
making it simple to identify what you see. Each bird gets a
full-page photograph paired with information ranging from
the bird's nest and eggs to favorite foods, as well as Stan's
fascinating naturalist notes.

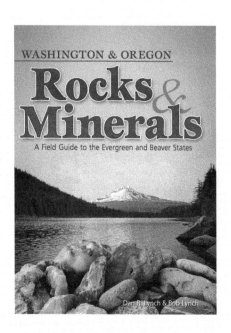

LEARN TO IDENTIFY ROCKS & MINERALS!

Rocks & Minerals of Washington & Oregon

Dan R. Lynch & Bob Lynch

**ISBN: 978-1-59193-293-2 • $14.95 • 4.38 x 6 • paperback
320 pages • full-color photos**

Get the perfect guide to minerals and rocks. This book features comprehensive entries for 124 Washington and Oregon rocks and minerals, from common rocks to rare finds. Learn from the fascinating information about everything from jasper and thunder eggs to gold and petrified wood. The easy-to-use format means you'll quickly find what you need to know and where to look. The authors' incredible, sharp, full-color photographs depict the detail needed for identification no need to guess from line drawings. With this field guide in hand, identifying and collecting is fun and informative.

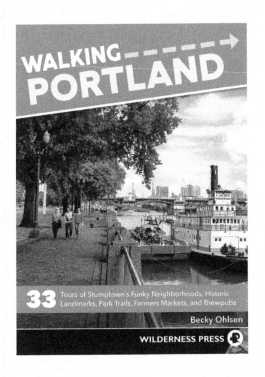

GET TO KNOW PORTLAND BY WALKING IT

Walking Portland

Becky Ohlsen

ISBN: 978-0-89997-892-5 • $16.95 • 5.5 x 7.5 • paperback
176 pages • full-color photos

Local author Becky Ohlsen guides you along 33 unique walking tours in this comprehensive book. Go beyond the obvious with self-guided tours that showcase hidden gardens, historic landmarks, award-winning restaurants, old-school taverns, oddball shops, and edgy warehouse galleries. Each featured walk includes full-color photographs and detailed neighborhood maps, along with vital public transportation and parking information. Route summaries highlight points of interest on each tour, while tips on where to dine, have a drink, and shop help to ensure that you find the "can't miss" locales. You'll soak up history, stories, and trivia.

About the Author

Stacy McCullough lives in Portland, OR with her husband, daughter, two cats and two dogs. She has spent over a decade—and counting—exploring and camping throughout the state; its "weirdness" and natural beauty draw her in. When she isn't taking road trips, Stacy can be found playing piano or guitar, getting her hands dirty in an attempt to keep a garden alive or playing a mean game of Connect 4.